Secrets of Amelia

An Experience in Cooking and History

McArthur Family Branch YMCA
YMCA of Florida's First Coast
Fernandina Beach, Florida

The McArthur Family Branch YMCA,
a local branch of the YMCA of Florida's First Coast,
ascribes to the Mission Statement:
*To put Christian principles into practice
through programs that build healthy spirit, mind and body for all.*

Proceeds from the sale of this book will be used to assist children and families
through the "Really Caring" financial assistance program.
Our goal is to never turn a child away from the YMCA
because of an inability to pay.

Additional copies may be obtained by addressing:

Secrets of Amelia

McArthur Family Branch YMCA
1915 Citrona Drive
Fernandina Beach, Florida 32034

Cover art: Judy Lott

Copyright© 1997 McArthur Family Branch YMCA

ISBN: 0-9656281-0-8

Manufactured in the United States of America
First Printing: 1997 5,000 copies

Designed, Edited and Manufactured by:
FRP™
P.O. Box 305142
Nashville, Tennessee 37230
1-800-358-0560

Book Design: Steve Newman

Introduction

Amelia Island, Florida, is a small, pristine barrier island. It is located on the East Coast, just south of the Georgia border and a few miles north of Jacksonville, Florida. First settled in 1562, it is packed with history and wonderful folklore. Amelia Island has been a haven for pirates and rum runners, the beginning of the railroad in Florida, and the port of call for the great sailing ships of both the nineteenth and early twentieth centuries. Fernandina was the site of grand "golden age" resorts, which attracted thousands of Americans and international visitors. The Island has flown the flags of eight different countries and was occupied by both the "Rebels" and the "Yankees" during the War Between the States.

It has been our goal to not only create a book of exceptional recipes, but to also share some of the colorful history that makes Amelia Island the unique place it is today. As you pore over *Secrets of Amelia* in your quest for one of its special recipes, we hope that you also enjoy the historical tidbits that are sprinkled throughout. By learning more about Amelia and the Victorian seaport town of Fernandina Beach, we are confident that you will agree that few places can compare to our island.

Many of the recipes in this book are truly best-kept secrets. They have been handed down from generation to generation and from friend to friend. Some have been pulled from cherished family cookbooks. All are tried and true and enjoyed by the Island contributors. We now present this collection to you in hopes that you will enjoy the dining secrets and pleasures that it offers.

Those who have given of their time and talents to the development of this book are pleased to share our dining treasures and our community with you. We are proud of our island home and even more pleased that your generosity, through the purchase of this book, will be of significant benefit to the children, youth, and families of our community. YOU HAVE MADE A DIFFERENCE TODAY IN THE LIFE OF A CHILD, AND WE THANK YOU!!

Cookbook Committee

Chairman—Shirley Owens   Executive Director—Jan C. Brogdon

Chris Bryan	Patty House	Amy Wampler
Ray Cline	June Peters	Melba Whitaker
Stephanie Hickox	Barbi Townsend	

About the Artist

Judy Lott's family graciously agreed to allow the YMCA to utilize her work as a final tribute to her and her love of this local community following her death in 1995. As with so many of Judy's designs, this watercolor truly depicts the ambiance of this small and historic island.

Judy's spirit and love of Amelia and its people are reflected in the art which she created during the last 20 years. Inspired by her environment she loved to say, "It's a watercolor morning."

Special Thanks

The YMCA is extremely grateful to our Board of Managers, members, volunteers, and staff for their support in the preparation and distribution of this book.

We would especially like to thank Winette Odom and Suanne Thamm of the Amelia Island Museum of History and "Amelia Now" for their assistance in compiling the historical details for this publication. If these morsels of history whet your appetite for more, the "grand banquet" is served at the museum, which is located in the old Nassau County jail in historic Fernandina Beach.

Contents

Early Beginnings

Appetizers

Native Americans

The Frenchman, Jean Ribault, landed on Amelia Island in May, 1562, and was met by the Timucuan Indians—tall, stately, and handsome people. The men were around seven feet tall and the women were about six feet tall. At one time there were probably in excess of twenty thousand Timucuans in north Florida from Cape Canaveral to just north of the St. Mary's River and west in a swath across to Tampa Bay.

The Timucuans, archaeologists have learned, evolved a pattern of life that remained constant for nearly two millennia. Their subsistence systems and material technology were in place by 500 B.C. It was the coming of the first Europeans that led to the ultimate extinction of these natives within a little more than a century. In addition to bringing "modern" weapons, they exposed the Timucuans to diseases for which the Indians had no immunity.

Much is known about these natives because of the writings of Jean Ribault and Rene de Laudonniere, plus work left by Jacques Le Moyne de Morgues, an artist and cartographer. Le Moyne made forty-three paintings depicting the everyday life of the Timucuans. A Flemish artist named Theodore Debry made engravings of these paintings, which he published in a book in 1591. Several reproductions from those early engravings are on display at the Amelia Island Museum of History.

Artichoke Loaf

You will love this easy dip for party fare. The "bowl" will be just as good as the dip in this recipe.

▼ Slice the top from the bread loaf. Scoop out the center, leaving a shell about ½ inch thick. Cut the top of the bread and the scooped out center into bite-size pieces.

▼ Butter the bottom of the bread shell lightly. Place on a foil-lined baking sheet. Sprinkle 1 cup of the cheese over the bottom of the shell.

▼ Drain the water-pack artichokes well; chop and layer over the cheese. Drain the chiles and layer over the artichokes.

▼ Drain the marinated artichokes, reserving about 1 teaspoon of the marinade. Chop the artichokes, mix with the reserved marinade and layer over the chiles.

▼ Spread the artichokes lightly with mayonnaise. Sprinkle with the remaining ½ cup cheese and paprika.

▼ Bake at 350 degrees for 30 minutes or until slightly bubbly.

▼ Serve with the bread cubes and tortilla chips for dipping. Toast the bread cubes if desired.

Yield: 8 to 10 servings

1 round bread loaf
2 tablespoons butter, softened
1½ cups shredded Cheddar cheese
2 (14-ounce) cans water-pack artichoke hearts
1 (4-ounce) can chopped green chiles
1 (6-ounce) jar marinated artichoke hearts
1 to 2 tablespoons mayonnaise
Paprika to taste
Tortilla chips

Black Bean Salsa

2 pounds dried black beans
1 ham bone
5 pounds tomatoes
2 red bell peppers
2 Bermuda onions
2 bunches fresh chives
1/2 cup chopped jalapeños
2/3 cup chopped fresh cilantro
1 teaspoon salt
2 teaspoons cumin
1/4 teaspoon cayenne
2/3 cup lime juice
2/3 cup virgin olive oil
Sour cream to taste
Tortilla chips or other corn chips

This recipe may sound somewhat weird but it is out-of-this-world good!

▼ Sort the beans and rinse well. Cook the beans with the ham bone according to the package directions until tender. Drain, rinse and drain well.

▼ Chop the tomatoes, red bell peppers, onions and chives.

▼ Combine with the jalapeños and cilantro in a large bowl. Add the beans and mix well.

▼ Add the salt, cumin, cayenne, lime juice and olive oil and mix well.

▼ Refrigerate, covered, for 24 hours or longer to allow the flavors to marry.

▼ Spoon the salsa into a serving bowl. Add a dollop of sour cream on top.

▼ Serve with tortilla chips for dipping.

Yield: 20 servings

Creamy Dill Dip for Vegetables

1 cup sour cream
1 cup mayonnaise
1 tablespoon dried minced onion
1 tablespoon dried dillweed
1/2 teaspoon seasoned salt
Bite-size fresh vegetables

▼ Blend the sour cream and mayonnaise in a medium bowl.

▼ Add the minced onion, dillweed and seasoned salt; mix well.

▼ Refrigerate, covered, for several hours to overnight.

▼ Serve with assorted bite-size fresh vegetables for dipping.

Yield: 2 cups

Chile Con Queso

▼ Cut the cheese into pieces. Combine the cheese, green chiles and pimentos in a double boiler.

▼ Cook over hot water until the cheese is melted, stirring frequently.

▼ Brown the sausage, ground round and onion in a large skillet, stirring until the meats are crumbly; drain well.

▼ Add the ground round mixture and the tomato to the cheese mixture. Cook over simmering water for 2 hours, stirring every 15 minutes.

▼ Pour into a chafing dish or slow cooker. Keep warm on Low. Serve with tortilla chips.

Yield: 16 servings

2 pounds Velveeta cheese
1 (4-ounce) can green chiles, drained, chopped
1 (2-ounce) jar chopped pimentos, drained
8 ounces hot sausage
1 pound ground round
1 large onion, chopped
1 medium tomato, chopped
1 (16-ounce) package tortilla chips or other corn chips

Easy Spinach Con Queso

▼ Place the spinach between paper towels and press until barely moist.

▼ Combine the cheese, milk, onion and pimentos in the top of a double boiler. Cook over hot water until the cheese is melted, stirring frequently.

▼ Stir in the spinach and tomato. Heat to serving temperature.

▼ Pour into a chafing dish. Keep warm on Low.

▼ Serve with tortilla chips.

Yield: 2 cups

1 (10-ounce) package frozen chopped spinach, thawed
1 pound Mexican-style Velveeta cheese, cubed
$1/2$ cup milk
1 small onion, chopped
1 (2-ounce) jar chopped pimentos, drained
1 medium tomato, chopped
1 (16-ounce) package tortilla chips

Guacamole

3 avocados, coarsely mashed
1 tablespoon lemon or lime juice
1 teaspoon Worcestershire sauce
2 medium tomatoes, peeled,
    seeded, chopped
1 teaspoon salt
1/8 teaspoon hot sauce
1 clove of garlic, crushed

▼ Combine the avocados, lemon juice and Worcestershire sauce in a bowl.
▼ Add the tomatoes, salt, hot sauce and garlic to the avocado mixture, mixing well.
▼ Spoon into a serving dish. Chill, covered, until serving time.
▼ Serve with corn chips for dipping or as a salad on a bed of shredded lettuce.

Yield: 8 servings

Shrimp Paste

3 pounds shrimp
Old Bay seasoning to taste
16 ounces cream cheese, softened
1 cup mayonnaise
1/2 cup finely chopped onion
Garlic salt to taste
Dry mustard to taste
Worcestershire sauce to taste

▼ Cook the shrimp with Old Bay seasoning in a large amount of boiling water in a saucepan. Drain, peel, devein and chop finely.
▼ Combine the cream cheese, mayonnaise and onion in a bowl and mix well. Stir in the shrimp. Season with garlic salt, dry mustard and Worcestershire sauce.
▼ Chill, covered, until serving time. May be made a day before serving to blend the flavors.
▼ Serve with club crackers.

Yield: 16 servings

Fried Dill Pickles

▼ Combine the egg, milk, Worcestershire sauce, Tabasco sauce, cayenne, garlic powder, salt and pepper in a bowl and mix well.

▼ Dip the pickle slices into the egg mixture to coat. Coat with the flour.

▼ Fry for 1 minute in hot oil in a skillet, turning to brown both sides. Drain on paper towels.

▼ Serve with fried fish.

Yield: 10 servings

1 egg
1 cup milk
2 teaspoons Worcestershire sauce
1/4 teaspoon Tabasco sauce
1/4 teaspoon cayenne
1/2 teaspoon garlic powder
Salt and pepper to taste
10 medium dill pickles, cut into
   1/4-inch slices
1 1/2 cups flour
Vegetable oil for frying

Spiced Pecans

▼ Butter or spray a baking sheet with nonstick cooking spray.

▼ Combine the egg white and cold water in a mixer bowl. Beat until foamy. Add the salt, sugar and cinnamon gradually, beating until stiff peaks form.

▼ Add the pecans, stirring until well-coated.

▼ Spread the pecans on the prepared baking sheet.

▼ Bake at 225 degrees for 45 minutes or until the pecans are dry and golden brown, stirring frequently.

Yield: 6 servings

1 egg white
1 tablespoon cold water
1/4 teaspoon salt
1/2 cup sugar
1/2 teaspoon cinnamon
3 cups pecan halves

Broiled Jumbo Shrimp with Mango Chutney

6 ounces soy sauce
1 teaspoon chopped fresh ginger
1 teaspoon chopped fresh garlic
1 ounce white wine
1 teaspoon mixed fresh herbs
4 to 6 jumbo shrimp per serving
Mango Chutney

This is one of the most requested appetizers served at the renowned Amelia Island Plantation. Prepare as many servings as you wish and enjoy!

▼ Combine the soy sauce, ginger, garlic, white wine and fresh herbs in a bowl and mix well. Add the shrimp. Marinate for about 1 minute, stirring occasionally.

▼ Sauté the shrimp in a skillet over high heat until lightly charred.

▼ Place the Mango Chutney in the center of a plate. Arrange the shrimp around the chutney. May top with a butter sauce and sprinkle with additional chopped fresh herbs.

Mango Chutney

4 ripe mangoes, seeded, thinly
   sliced
1/2 red bell pepper, finely chopped
8 ounces raisins
1/2 cup apple cider vinegar
1/2 cup packed brown sugar
1 teaspoon nutmeg
1 teaspoon ground cloves

▼ Combine the mangoes, red pepper, raisins, vinegar, brown sugar, nutmeg and cloves in a bowl and toss to mix.

▼ Chill, covered, for 8 to 10 hours.

   Yield: variable

Dilled Shrimp

▼ Sauté the garlic and scallions lightly in butter and olive oil in a large skillet.

▼ Add the shrimp. Sauté over medium heat for 3 minutes or until the shrimp turn pink.

▼ Add the lemon juice, finely chopped dill, salt and pepper, stirring to mix.

▼ Serve warm or cold garnished with dill sprigs and lemon slices.

Yield: 8 servings

1 tablespoon minced garlic
2 tablespoons minced scallions
2 tablespoons melted butter or margarine
1 tablespoon olive oil
1¾ pounds large fresh shrimp, peeled, deveined
2 tablespoons lemon juice
4 teaspoons finely chopped fresh dill
⅛ teaspoon salt
⅛ teaspoon pepper
Dill sprigs
Lemon slices

Old Town

Fernandina's early history centers around the riverfront area on the north end of Amelia Island known as Old Town. To find Old Town, take North 14th Street past Bosque Bello cemetery, turn left onto White Street, and go four blocks to Plaza San Carlos.

Indians camped over a period from 2000 to 1000 B.C., and Spanish missionaries plied their trade as early as the sixteenth century in this area. The English cultivated indigo in the eighteenth century, and here, the Spanish town of Fernandina (named for Ferdinand VII, King of Spain) was founded in 1811. It is Florida's only Spanish town for which the original site plan remains.

Marinated Shrimp

1¼ cups olive oil
¾ cup vinegar
2½ tablespoons capers
2½ teaspoons celery seeds
1½ teaspoons salt
7 bay leaves
Hot sauce to taste
1 medium onion, sliced
5 pounds medium shrimp, peeled,
    cooked

▼ Combine the olive oil, vinegar, capers, celery seeds, salt, bay leaves, hot sauce and onion in a shallow bowl and mix well. Add the shrimp, stirring to coat.

▼ Marinate, covered, in the refrigerator for 8 hours or longer, stirring occasionally.

▼ Remove the bay leaves before serving.

Yield: 20 servings

Cheese Straws

1½ cups grated sharp Cheddar
    cheese
½ cup butter, softened
1½ cups flour
1 teaspoon baking powder
1 teaspoon sugar
½ teaspoon salt
1 teaspoon cayenne

▼ Blend the cheese and butter in a bowl until smooth and light.

▼ Combine the dry ingredients and add to the cheese mixture. Mix until smooth.

▼ Force the mixture through a cookie press fitted with the star plate to make long ropes of dough on ungreased cookie sheets. Cut into 2-inch-long pieces.

▼ Bake at 350 degrees for 15 to 20 minutes or just until the straws begin to brown.

Yield: 2 to 3 dozen

Zucchini Hors d'Oeuvre

▼ Combine the biscuit mix, onion, cheese, parsley, salt, seasoned salt, oregano, pepper, garlic, oil and eggs in a bowl and mix well.

▼ Add the zucchini and stir gently until well coated.

▼ Spread the mixture evenly in a lightly greased 9x13-inch baking pan.

▼ Bake at 350 degrees for 30 minutes or until golden brown.

▼ Let stand for about 5 minutes before cutting into 1½-inch squares. Serve warm.

Yield: 48 servings

1 cup biscuit mix
½ cup finely chopped onion
½ cup grated Parmesan cheese
2 tablespoons chopped fresh parsley
½ teaspoon salt
½ teaspoon seasoned salt
½ teaspoon ground oregano
⅛ teaspoon pepper
1 clove of garlic, minced
¼ cup vegetable oil
4 eggs, beaten
3 cups grated zucchini

The Timucuans

The Timucuans were a friendly, honest, and diligent people. They apparently maintained a harmonious lifestyle in union with nature, living on an island they called Napoyca.

One custom of the Timucuans was tattooing. This was a privilege bestowed on men and women of prominence in their tribe. Red, black, yellow, and blue colors were tattooed on their faces, chests, stomachs, and thighs, which gave a false appearance of ferocity.

The Melting Pot

Soups & Sauces

Four Hundred Years Under Eight Flags

Amelia Island is Florida's Golden Isle, which the French visited, the Spanish developed, the English named, and the Americans tamed. It is the only U.S. location to have been under eight different flags.

French, 1562–1565—The Frenchman, Jean Ribault, landed on the island on May 3, 1562, and named it Isle de Mai. Jean Ribault was the island's first recorded European visitor.

Spanish, 1565–1763—After defeating the French, the Spanish renamed the island Santa Maria after its mission. Both mission and settlement were destroyed in 1702 by the English. James Oglethorpe, Governor of Georgia, renamed the island Amelia for the daughter of George II.

English, 1763–1783—The island became known as Egmont because of the Earl of Egmont's large indigo plantation.

Spanish, 1783–1821 (with three interruptions)—Britain ceded Florida back to Spain after the Revolution. The Embargo Act of 1807 closed U.S. ports to foreign shipment and made Fernandina a center of activity for smugglers and pirates.

Patriots—The "Patriots of Amelia Island" overthrew the Spanish and raised their flag on March 17, 1812. The next day it was replaced by the U.S. flag but Spain demanded that the island be returned.

Green Cross of Florida—The island was seized in June, 1817, by Gregor MacGregor. When he withdrew, the Spanish tried to regain the island but were repelled by forces under Jared Irwin and Ruggles Hubbard.

Mexican Rebel Flag—Pirate Luis Aury gained control and hoisted the Mexican flag. In December, 1817, the U.S. occupied the island and held it "in trust for Spain."

United States, 1821—Present (with one interruption)—In 1821 Spain ceded the island to the U.S.

Confederate, 1861–1862—Confederate troops seized control of the island in April, 1861, and held it until March, 1862, when Federal troops recaptured it and occupied the island for the duration of the War Between the States.

Barbecued Bean Soup

This is a sturdy soup which is portable and adaptable. It loves to settle into a thermos and wait. (You know you've been fed when you've had this.) It is great hot, lukewarm or cold.

▼ Combine the ground chuck, green peppers and onions in a large skillet. Cook until the ground chuck is brown, stirring until crumbly.

▼ Drain the ground chuck mixture well and place in a large soup pot.

▼ Add the beans, pineapple, barbecue sauce and seasonings and mix well.

▼ Cook, covered, over low heat for 1 hour, stirring occasionally.

Yield: 10 servings

2 pounds ground chuck
2 green bell peppers, chopped
2 onions, chopped
1 (16-ounce) can kidney beans, drained
2 (16-ounce) cans Campbell's pork and beans
1 (16-ounce) jar B & M baked beans
2 (16-ounce) cans crushed pineapple
1 (18-ounce) jar Heinz 100 percent natural thick and rich barbecue sauce
Brown sugar, mustard, vinegar and ketchup to taste

Black Bean Soup

⅔ cup chopped onion
4 cloves of garlic, minced
1 tablespoon ground cumin
½ to 1 teaspoon crushed red
   pepper flakes
2 tablespoons vegetable oil
4 (16-ounce) cans black beans
1½ cups chicken broth
3 cups mild or medium thick and
   chunky salsa
2 tablespoons lime juice
½ cup nonfat plain yogurt or sour
   cream

▼ Sauté the onion and garlic with the cumin and red pepper flakes in oil in a 4-quart soup pot over medium heat until the onion is tender. Remove from the heat.

▼ Process 2 or 3 cans of the undrained beans and the chicken broth in a blender until puréed. Add to the soup pot and mix well.

▼ Stir in the remaining undrained beans, salsa and lime juice. Bring to a boil, stirring occasionally. Reduce the heat to a simmer.

▼ Cook, covered, over low heat for 30 minutes, stirring occasionally.

▼ Ladle into bowls. Top with a dollop of yogurt or sour cream. Serve with crackers.

▼ The soup will have a thicker consistency if 3 cans of beans are puréed.

Yield: 12 servings

School Bells Ring on Amelia

In 1567, Pedro Menendez, Spanish governor of Florida, came to the island, built a fort, and established a mission. The native Timucuan Indians proved to be more receptive to the ways of the white man than any of the other Florida tribes. Santa Maria mission was established between 1597 and 1602 and was one of a chain of coastal Catholic missions extending north as far as Port Royal, South Carolina. Many of the Timucuans soon were converted to Christianity and for more than one hundred years the priests worked among the Indians teaching them to read and write. Grammars, catechisms, and other books were written in the native language as early as 1602.

Meatball, Escarole and Kidney Bean Soup

▼ Combine the ground chuck, eggs, cheese, bread crumbs, basil, salt and pepper in a bowl and mix well. Shape into 2-inch meatballs.

▼ Heat the olive oil in a 6-quart soup pot. Add the meatballs. Cook until brown on all sides.

▼ Remove the meatballs to a warm bowl. Keep warm.

▼ Sauté the onion in the pan drippings in the stockpot until tender. Add the chicken stock.

▼ Separate and rinse the escarole. Drain and break into bite-size pieces. Add to the stockpot.

▼ Cook for 20 minutes or until the escarole is tender.

▼ Add the meatballs and beans.

▼ Cook just until heated through, stirring occasionally.

Yield: 6 servings

1 pound lean ground chuck
2 eggs
1/2 cup grated Parmesan cheese
1/2 cup seasoned bread crumbs
3 tablespoons chopped fresh basil
1/4 teaspoon salt
1/4 teaspoon pepper
3 tablespoons olive oil
1 large onion, chopped
6 cups chicken stock
1 (1-pound) head escarole
3 cups cooked red kidney beans

Indian Burial Mounds

William Bartram, noted botanist, landed on the northern coast of the island in March 1776. Interested in archeology as well as other features of the area, Bartram wrote, "On Egmont estate are several very large Indian tumuli, which are called Ogeechee mounds, so named from that nation of Indians who took shelter here, after being driven from their native settlements on the mainland near Ogeechee River. Here they were constantly harassed by the Carolinians and Creeks, and at length slain by their conquerors, and their bones entombed in these heaps of earth and shells." The location is in Fernandina Beach between the present North Twelfth and Thirteenth Streets where the Nassau County Board of Education building now sits.

Corn Chowder

4 slices bacon
1 medium onion, sliced
4 cups cubed peeled potatoes
1 cup water
4 cups whole kernel corn
1 cup light cream
1 teaspoon sugar
1/4 cup butter or margarine, cut
  into pieces
2 teaspoons salt
1/4 teaspoon pepper
2 cups milk

▼ Chop the bacon into small pieces.
▼ Sauté the bacon and onion in a soup pot until the bacon is crisp and golden brown.
▼ Add the potatoes and water. Bring to a boil over medium heat, stirring occasionally. Reduce the heat.
▼ Cook, covered, over low heat for 10 minutes, stirring occasionally.
▼ Add the corn, cream, sugar, butter, salt, pepper and milk and mix well.
▼ Heat to serving temperature, stirring frequently. Do not allow the soup to boil.

Yield: 8 servings

The Bullfight

In 1815 Don Domingo Fernandez, owner of the land on which the present-day city of Fernandina was built, granted permission to Captain Pangua, commandant of Fort San Carlos, to hold a festival in honor of Dona Isabel, daughter of the "Contador," in a grove on one of his plantations. The uninvited locals were a bit scandalized that the festivities, which included a lavish banquet and a ball, were held on a Sunday. But imagine how the tongues must have wagged when, after the feast, guests were led to a sawdust-filled arena surrounded by tiers of seats. According to an 1890 recounting of events, "At a given signal, a young Spaniard, dressed a la matador, entered with the conventional red flags, being afoot, however, and armed only with a stiletto. After awhile, a half-grown bull of fierce aspect but insignificant weight was turned in and the sport began. The red flags were shaken in the face of the bull, which plunged wildly at the matador, who got in a number of sharp wounds on the sides and flanks of the enraged animal." The fight was ultimately declared a draw. The bull left the arena bloody, but not seriously hurt. And thus ended the only bullfight ever recorded in Florida.

*M*inestrone

▼ Combine the beef, water, undrained tomatoes, bouillon cube, onion, parsley, salt, thyme and pepper in a 4-quart slow cooker and mix well.

▼ Cook, covered, on Low for 7 to 9 hours or until the beef is tender. It is not necessary to stir during cooking.

▼ Increase the heat to High.

▼ Add the zucchini, cabbage, beans and macaroni. Cook, covered, for 30 to 45 minutes or until the vegetables are tender.

▼ Ladle into soup bowls. Sprinkle with Parmesan cheese.

Yield: 8 servings

1 pound lean beef stew meat
6 cups water
1 (28-ounce) can tomatoes, chopped
1 beef bouillon cube
1 medium onion, chopped
2 tablespoons minced dried parsley
2 teaspoons salt
1½ teaspoons ground thyme
½ teaspoon pepper
1 medium zucchini, thinly sliced
2 cups finely chopped cabbage
1 (16-ounce) can garbanzo beans, drained
1 cup uncooked small elbow or shell macaroni
¼ cup grated Parmesan cheese

Caramelized Onion Broth with Thyme Crostini

10 whole Vidalia onions
Salt and pepper to taste
2 tablespoons olive oil
1 cup white wine
4 cups chicken stock
1 cup water
2 bay leaves
¹/₂ bunch fresh thyme sprigs
5 peppercorns
**2 tablespoons chopped fresh
  thyme**
2 tablespoons butter, softened
**2 tablespoons grated Parmesan
  cheese**
1 small baguette

*Dining at the Ritz Carlton is truly an elegant experience.
This recipe given by the Ritz is one we think you'll find
very appealing.*

▼ Peel the onions and cut julienne-style. Cook the onions
  with salt and pepper in hot olive oil in a soup pot for 30
  minutes or until caramelized, stirring frequently.

▼ Deglaze the soup pot with the white wine.

▼ Add the chicken stock and water.

▼ Tie the bay leaves, thyme sprigs and peppercorns in a
  cheesecloth bag. Add to the soup pot.

▼ Simmer, covered, for 45 minutes, stirring occasionally.

▼ Combine the chopped thyme, butter and Parmesan
  cheese in a bowl and mix well.

▼ Cut the baguette into thin slices. Spread the thyme
  mixture on the baguette slices. Place on a baking sheet.

▼ Toast the crostini under a hot broiler.

▼ Remove the cheesecloth bundle of herbs. Ladle the broth
  into serving bowls. Float the hot crostini on the broth.

Yield: 6 servings

Creamy Shrimp and Cauliflower Soup

Thanks to K. P.'s Deli for this great soup recipe. "Something different in a deli" can be found at K. P.'s.

▼ Sauté the onions in the margarine in a soup pot until tender. Add the flour gradually, mixing well to make a roux.

▼ Stir in the milk gradually. Cook until thickened, stirring constantly.

▼ Steam the cauliflower and shrimp together in a steamer over boiling water until the cauliflower is tender-crisp. Drain, reserving 2 cups of the cooking liquid.

▼ Add the cauliflower and shrimp to the soup and mix well.

▼ Dissolve the bouillon cubes in the reserved cooking liquid. Add to the soup.

▼ Cook over medium heat until heated to serving temperature, stirring frequently.

Yield: 20 servings

2 medium onions, chopped
1 cup margarine
2 cups flour
16 cups (1 gallon) milk
Florets of 2 heads cauliflower
2 pounds peeled deveined shrimp
4 chicken bouillon cubes

Split Pea Soup

3 cups dried split peas
1 meaty ham bone
6 cups water
1 teaspoon salt

▼ Sort and rinse the split peas.
▼ Combine the split peas and enough water to cover in a large soup pot. Let stand, covered, for 8 to 10 hours.
▼ Drain the peas. Add the ham bone, 6 cups water and salt. Bring to a boil over medium heat.
▼ Cook, covered, over low heat for 3 hours, stirring occasionally.
▼ Remove the ham bone. Cut the meat from the bone. Add the meat to the soup and discard the bone.
▼ Simmer, uncovered, for 40 minutes, stirring occasionally.
▼ Pour a small amount of soup at a time into a blender container. Process until puréed. Return the puréed soup to the soup pot.
▼ Heat to serving temperature.

Yield: 8 servings

Summer Fruit Soup

3 cantaloupes
2 cups strawberries
1/2 cup orange juice
2 cups vanilla yogurt
1 cup raspberries
8 mint sprigs

▼ Cut the rind from the cantaloupes and scoop out and discard the seeds. Cut the cantaloupe pulp into pieces.
▼ Rinse the strawberries, remove the hulls and cut the strawberries into halves.
▼ Combine the cantaloupes, strawberries and orange juice in a blender container. Process until puréed.
▼ Reserve 1/2 cup of the yogurt. Add the remaining yogurt to the blender and process until smooth.
▼ Pour the soup into bowls. Top each serving with 1 tablespoon of the reserved yogurt, a few raspberries and a sprig of mint.

Yield: 8 servings

Summer Vegetable Soup

▼ Sauté the onion in the oil in a soup pot for 3 to 4 minutes.

▼ Add the chicken broth, bay leaf, basil leaves, parsley, lemon zest, tomatoes, carrots, potatoes, celery, salt and pepper.

▼ Bring to a boil over medium heat and reduce the heat to low.

▼ Simmer, covered, for 20 minutes, stirring occasionally.

▼ Add the corn, green beans and zucchini.

▼ Simmer, covered, for 15 minutes longer, stirring occasionally.

▼ Discard the bay leaf, parsley and lemon zest.

▼ Ladle the soup into bowls.

Yield: 4 servings

1 medium onion, chopped
2 tablespoons vegetable oil
6 cups chicken broth
1 bay leaf
3 fresh basil leaves
2 fresh parsley sprigs
2 (2-inch) strips lemon zest
1 pound tomatoes, chopped
1 cup thinly sliced carrots
2 cups (1-inch) cubes unpeeled
    red potatoes
½ cup chopped celery
½ teaspoon salt
Freshly ground pepper to taste
Kernels of 1 ear yellow corn or
    1 cup frozen corn
1 cup diagonally-cut green beans
1 cup julienne zucchini

Gregor MacGregor

The man responsible for the Green Cross of Florida flag that flew briefly over Amelia Island was a flamboyant Scotsman named Gregor MacGregor. Born in 1786, young Gregor, as adventurous as he was skilled in things military, quit the structured life of the British army to make his fortune in South America.

MacGregor had developed a hatred for Spain as a result of his adventures in South America and decided to move against the Spanish in Florida. MacGregor recruited about 150 dubious characters from the waterfronts along the East Coast to form his Florida invasion force. Recognizing that his men would never constitute a well-disciplined fighting force, MacGregor decided that a successful invasion could only come about through trickery and subterfuge. On June 18, 1817, MacGregor sent word via a small group of fishermen to the commandant of Fernandina's Fort San Carlos: Brigadier General Gregor MacGregor was on his way to invade Amelia Island with several large ships and a thousand troops—but if he encountered no opposition, no one would be harmed.

This message struck fear into Colonel Francisco Morales, who quickly decided that there was no way the Spanish could prevail against such odds. The next day MacGregor's invasionary force of less than 100 men landed on the island's north end. Morales, convinced that this motley crew was just the advance guard of a large force hidden in the woods, quickly surrendered.

MacGregor planted his Green Cross of Florida flag over Fort San Carlos and issued a special proclamation congratulating his men on their decisive victory. Within his first week in Fernandina, MacGregor had organized a government and set up shop to handle the booty and prize goods of all the privateers and pirates whom he invited to make their home in Fernandina. MacGregor's financial backers quickly lost confidence in the Scottish adventurer when his unpaid troops started plundering coastal settlements both in Florida and Georgia. Just two months after taking command, MacGregor resigned his government and sailed away with the tide, never to be seen on Amelia Island again.

North Carolina Barbecue Sauce

This is a delicious non-tomato-style barbecue sauce

▼ Combine the vinegars, sugar, red pepper flakes, Tabasco sauce, salt and black pepper in a bowl and mix well.
▼ Let stand for several hours for the flavors to blend.
▼ Use this sauce to season slow-cooked chopped or shredded pork roast to serve on hamburger buns with coleslaw.

Yield: 2 cups

1 cup cider vinegar
1 cup white vinegar
1 tablespoon sugar
1 tablespoon hot red pepper flakes
1 tablespoon (or less) Tabasco sauce
Salt and black pepper to taste

Dijon Grilling Sauce

▼ Combine the mayonnaise, milk, mustard, honey and salt in a bowl and mix well.
▼ Store, covered, in the refrigerator for up to 1 week.
▼ Brush some of the sauce on fish while grilling or broiling, then serve the remaining sauce on the side.

Yield: 1¼ cups

½ cup light mayonnaise
⅓ cup skim milk
¼ cup coarse-grain Dijon mustard
2 tablespoons honey
Salt to taste

Honey-Mustard Sauce

½ cup honey
1 cup mustard
¼ cup mayonnaise

▼ Combine the honey, mustard and mayonnaise in a bowl and mix well.
▼ Store in a covered container in the refrigerator.
▼ This is a great sauce for chicken tenders.

Yield: 1¾ cups

No-Fail Hollandaise Sauce

2 egg yolks
½ cup butter
Juice of 1 medium lemon

This is a great recipe for asparagus, broccoli, eggs Benedict, artichokes and to make you very FAT!

▼ Combine the egg yolks, butter and lemon juice in a saucepan at room temperature. Place the saucepan over medium-high heat.
▼ Cook until the sauce is thickened, whisking constantly. The sauce will separate if you stop whisking too soon.
▼ Do not substitute margarine for the butter in this recipe.

Yield: ¾ cup

Janice's Special Meat Marinade

1 (10-ounce) bottle light soy sauce
⅓ cup packed brown sugar
1 teaspoon dry mustard
1 teaspoon ginger
½ teaspoon garlic powder

This is great for marinating kabobs or any kind of meat.

▼ Combine the soy sauce, brown sugar, mustard, ginger and garlic powder in a bowl and mix well.
▼ Add the meat of choice and mix or turn until the meat is well coated with the marinade.
▼ Marinate, covered, in the refrigerator until ready to cook.

Yield: 1½ cups

Bill's Famous Teriyaki Marinade

This is a good marinade for meat, especially boneless pork tenders or steaks.

▼ Combine the teriyaki sauce, soy sauce, oyster sauce, oil, vinegar, garlic, gingerroot and onion powder in a bowl and mix well.

▼ Combine the meat of choice and the marinade in a large sealable plastic bag. Marinate in the refrigerator for 8 to 10 hours.

▼ Drain and discard the marinade. Grill the meat as desired.

Yield: 3/4 cup

1/2 **cup teriyaki sauce**
1 **tablespoon soy sauce**
1 **tablespoon oyster sauce**
1 **tablespoon sesame oil**
1 **tablespoon rice wine vinegar**
1/2 **teaspoon chopped garlic**
1/2 **teaspoon freshly grated gingerroot**
1/2 **teaspoon onion powder**

Mango Salsa

Use this delightful mixture as a salsa or to top chicken breasts, turkey cutlets or baked or broiled fish for the last few minutes of cooking.

▼ Combine the mango, tomato, red onion, green onions, cilantro, olive oil, lime juice and jalapeño in a bowl and mix well. Add salt and pepper and mix well.

▼ May prepare the salsa just before serving or several hours before serving time and chill in the refrigerator.

Yield: 3 1/4 cups

1 **cup cubed peeled mango**
1 **cup chopped seeded tomato**
1/2 **cup finely chopped red onion**
1/4 **cup finely chopped green onions**
2 **tablespoons chopped cilantro**
2 **tablespoons olive oil**
2 **tablespoons lime juice**
1 **jalapeño, seeded, finely chopped**
Salt and pepper to taste

Hearty Fare

Breakfast & Breads

Pirates

$\mathcal{B}$eginning in the early 1600s and lasting for about two hundred years, Amelia Island saw many of the world's pirates sail into its harbor. There were pirates, privateers, and buccaneers, with fine lines of distinction between each. In 1807, the United States closed its ports to foreign shipping so Fernandina, not part of the United States, became the busiest port in the Western Hemisphere. It was a Spanish border town through which anything could be smuggled into the United States.

The most documented pirate to come to these shores was Luis Aury. He was born in Paris in 1788 and became a French privateer after a brief stint with the French Navy. In 1813, he sailed as a privateer for Cartagena and later for the cause of the Mexican rebels. In September 1817, Aury "annexed" Amelia Island to the Mexican republic. Two months later he trained the guns of his privateers on Fernandina and declared himself supreme civil and military authority.

President Monroe invoked a secret act that had been passed in 1811 that gave the President power to expel by force any foreign power occupying Spanish Florida. Aury surrendered to United States forces on December 23, 1817. As the Mexican flag was lowered, the United States assumed control of Amelia Island, holding it in trust for the Spanish.

Bacon Broccoli Quiche

▼ Cook the bacon in a skillet until crisp and drain on paper towels.

▼ Combine the butter and cracker crumbs in a bowl and mix well. Press over the bottom of an 8-inch springform pan.

▼ Combine the Swiss cheese and ricotta cheese in a bowl and mix well. Add the eggs 1 at a time, mixing well after each addition. Add the bacon, broccoli and onion and mix well. Pour into the prepared pan. Sprinkle with nutmeg.

▼ Bake at 350 degrees for 1 hour or until the center is set.

▼ Sprinkle with the Parmesan cheese. Let stand for 10 minutes before serving.

Yield: 6 servings

1 pound bacon, cut into $1/2$-inch pieces
3 tablespoons melted butter
$1^1/_4$ cups rye cracker crumbs
$1^1/_2$ cups shredded Swiss cheese
15 ounces ricotta cheese
4 eggs
1 (10-ounce) package frozen chopped broccoli, thawed
1 small onion, chopped
Nutmeg to taste
2 tablespoons grated Parmesan cheese

The Golden Isle

Amelia Islanders are convinced that this is the "most golden" of the Golden Isles. It's logical for our woods and hammocks to hoard pirate treasure because, over a two-hundred-year period, this area attracted the largest concentration of sea thieves in America. Even the island's Supreme Commander at one time, Luis Aury, was a pirate by trade. Political pressure forced Aury to leave in such haste that he had to leave his treasure behind . . . somewhere.

Overnight Breakfast Casserole

8 ounces sausage
6 eggs
2 cups milk
1 teaspoon salt
¹⁄₈ teaspoon dry mustard
4 slices bread, cubed
1 cup shredded Cheddar cheese

▼ Brown the sausage in a skillet, stirring until crumbly, and drain.

▼ Combine the eggs, milk, salt and mustard in a mixer bowl and beat well.

▼ Layer the bread cubes, sausage, cheese and egg mixture in a 9x13-inch baking dish.

▼ Chill, covered, for 8 to 10 hours.

▼ Bake at 400 degrees for 25 to 30 minutes or until light brown.

Yield: 4 servings

Follow the Rules

A vast amount of superstition surrounds the pursuit of buried booty. This characteristic was colorfully described by Lew Dietz in his article, "Florida's Fabulous Treasure Bay" in the August 1962 *Argosy*:

"Treasures are very apt to be protected by guardian ghosts, and black-hearted buccaneers make most unsavory haunts. To get anywhere at all under these circumstances, a man should have complete command of the Book of Moses and a good supply of special-delivery oil. A man digging for treasure should never talk on the job, nor should he sweat inordinately. Moreover, he must swear off tobacco and liquor and women for four days."

Country Breakfast Casserole

This is a great recipe for "company breakfast" or brunch.
Serve with fruit and muffins for a great day starter.

▼ Brown the sausage in a skillet, stirring until crumbly;
  drain.
▼ Combine the water and salt in a large saucepan. Bring to
  a boil over medium heat. Stir in the grits gradually. Cook
  over low heat for 4 to 5 minutes, stirring frequently.
▼ Add the eggs, 1 cup of the cheese, milk, margarine and
  pepper and mix well. Stir in the sausage. Pour into a
  buttered 2-quart baking dish. Sprinkle with the remaining
  ½ cup cheese.
▼ Bake at 350 degrees for 1 hour. Serve hot.

  Yield: 6 servings

1 pound bulk sausage
4 cups water
1 teaspoon salt
1 cup grits
4 eggs, slightly beaten
1½ cups shredded Cheddar
   cheese
1 cup milk
½ cup margarine
Pepper to taste

Breakfast Burritos

▼ Blend the sour cream and taco seasoning mix in a small
  bowl. Set aside.
▼ Beat the eggs with the water in a small bowl until
  well blended.
▼ Preheat a large skillet sprayed with nonstick cooking
  spray over medium-low heat. Add the beaten eggs. Cook
  until set, stirring occasionally.
▼ Spread the tortillas with the sour cream mixture. Divide
  the eggs, cheese, romaine and tomato among the tortillas
  and roll up tightly. Serve immediately.

  Yield: 6 servings

¾ cup sour cream
2 tablespoons taco seasoning mix
6 eggs
2 tablespoons water
6 (8-inch) flour tortillas, warmed
¾ cup shredded Cheddar cheese
1 cup shredded romaine
1 medium tomato, seeded,
   chopped

Blackberry Coffee Cake

1/2 cup butter, softened
1 cup sugar
3 eggs, slightly beaten
1 teaspoon baking powder
1/4 teaspoon salt
1 teaspoon baking soda
2 cups flour
1 cup sour cream
2 cups fresh or frozen
   blackberries
1 cup packed brown sugar
1/4 cup butter, softened
1/4 cup flour

▼ Cream 1/2 cup butter and sugar in a mixer bowl. Add the eggs, baking powder, salt and baking soda and beat well.

▼ Add 2 cups flour alternately with the sour cream, beating well after each addition. Fold in the blackberries.

▼ Pour into a buttered 9x13-inch baking pan.

▼ Beat the brown sugar and remaining 1/4 cup butter in a mixer bowl until creamy. Add 1/4 cup flour and mix until crumbly. Sprinkle over the batter.

▼ Bake at 350 degrees for 30 minutes or until the coffee cake tests done. The topping should melt and partially sink into the batter.

▼ May substitute blueberries or strawberries for the blackberries.

Yield: 12 servings

Yogurt Pecan Coffee Cake

A dab of yogurt makes this coffee cake just as rich and moist as your grandmother's but with less fat and fewer calories. It complements any hot beverage, morning, noon or night.

▼ Sift the flours, baking powder, baking soda and salt together and set aside.

▼ Combine the maple syrup and ⅓ cup oil in a mixer bowl and beat until blended. Add the eggs, yogurt and vanilla and blend well.

▼ Add the flour mixture and beat just until combined and evenly moistened.

▼ Spread half the batter in an oiled 9-inch-round or -square baking pan.

▼ Combine the pecans, brown sugar, cinnamon and remaining ¼ cup oil in a bowl and mix until crumbly. Sprinkle half the pecan mixture over the batter in the baking pan. Spread the remaining batter on top. Sprinkle with the remaining pecan mixture.

▼ Bake at 350 degrees for 40 to 45 minutes or until the coffee cake tests done.

▼ Cool in the pan on a wire rack for 10 minutes before cutting.

Yield: 9 servings

1 cup whole wheat pastry flour
1 cup unbleached flour
1 teaspoon baking powder
1 teaspoon baking soda
¼ teaspoon salt
½ cup maple syrup
⅓ cup canola oil
2 eggs, beaten
1 cup plain nonfat yogurt
1 teaspoon vanilla extract
1 cup finely chopped, lightly toasted pecans
¼ cup packed brown sugar
1 teaspoon cinnamon
¼ cup canola oil

Nutty Coffee Cake

1 egg, beaten
1/2 cup sugar
1/2 cup milk
2 tablespoons melted butter
1 cup flour
1/2 teaspoon salt
2 teaspoons baking powder
1/4 cup packed brown sugar
1 teaspoon cinnamon
1 tablespoon flour
1 tablespoon melted butter
1/2 cup chopped pecans

▼ Combine the egg, sugar, milk and 2 tablespoons butter in a mixer bowl and beat well.
▼ Sift 1 cup flour, salt and baking powder together. Add to the batter, mixing well. Pour into a greased 8-inch square baking pan.
▼ Combine the brown sugar, cinnamon, 1 tablespoon flour and remaining 1 tablespoon butter in a bowl. Mix until crumbly. Stir in the pecans. Sprinkle over the batter.
▼ Bake at 375 degrees for 20 to 25 minutes or until the coffee cake tests done.

Yield: 8 servings

Baked Hush Puppies

2/3 cup yellow cornmeal
1/3 cup flour
1 teaspoon baking powder
1/2 teaspoon salt
1/2 cup minced onion
1/3 cup skim milk
1/4 cup egg substitute
1 tablespoon vegetable oil
1/8 teaspoon pepper

▼ Combine the cornmeal, flour, baking powder, salt and onion in a medium bowl and mix well. Make a well in the center.
▼ Combine the skim milk, egg substitute, oil and pepper in a small bowl and mix well.
▼ Add the milk mixture to the flour mixture and mix just until moistened.
▼ Fill miniature muffin cups sprayed with nonstick cooking spray 3/4 full with the batter.
▼ Bake at 450 degrees for 12 to 15 minutes or until golden brown. Remove from the pans immediately and serve hot.

Yield: 2 dozen hush puppies

Broccoli Corn Bread

▼ Combine the corn bread mix, onion, eggs and butter in a bowl and mix well.
▼ Drain the broccoli. Stir the broccoli, cottage cheese and Cheddar cheese into the batter. Pour into a greased 9x13-inch baking pan.
▼ Bake at 375 degrees for 40 minutes or until golden brown.

Yield: 12 servings

2 (7-ounce) packages corn bread mix
1 onion, chopped
5 eggs
¾ cup melted butter
1 (10-ounce) package frozen chopped broccoli, thawed
8 ounces cottage cheese
1 cup shredded Cheddar cheese

Southern Corn Bread

This is a very old recipe that is wonderful served with vegetables.

▼ Preheat a greased 10-inch ovenproof skillet.
▼ Sift the cornmeal, flour, salt and baking soda into a bowl. Add the buttermilk, egg and bacon drippings and mix just until the dry ingredients are moistened.
▼ Pour the batter into the prepared skillet.
▼ Bake at 450 degrees for 20 to 25 minutes or until golden brown.
▼ Serve warm with butter.

Yield: 6 servings

1½ cups enriched white cornmeal
3 tablespoons flour
1 teaspoon salt
1 teaspoon baking soda
2 cups buttermilk
1 egg
2 tablespoons bacon drippings or melted butter

Jalapeño Corn Bread

1½ cups cornmeal
1 tablespoon (heaping) flour
1 teaspoon salt
½ teaspoon baking soda
1 cup buttermilk
⅔ cup vegetable oil
2 eggs, beaten
3 to 6 jalapeños, chopped
½ green bell pepper, chopped
4 to 5 green onions, chopped
1½ cups shredded Cheddar
    cheese

▼ Combine the cornmeal, flour, salt and baking soda in a bowl and mix well. Add the buttermilk, oil and eggs and mix well.
▼ Stir in the jalapeños, green bell pepper, green onions and cheese.
▼ Pour into a greased 9x13-inch baking dish.
▼ Bake at 375 degrees for 35 minutes or until golden brown.

Yield: 12 servings

"Pop Pop's Mush"

1½ cups cold water
1½ cups cornmeal
3 cups boiling water

▼ Combine the cold water and cornmeal in a bowl and mix well. Stir into the boiling water in a saucepan. Cook, covered, over medium-low heat for 30 minutes, stirring occasionally.
▼ Pour into a greased 5x9-inch loaf pan. Let the mixture stand until cool and set.
▼ Store, covered, in the refrigerator.
▼ Cut the mush into slices and brown on a hot griddle. Serve warm with syrup.

Yield: 10 slices

Banana Nut Bread

▼ Cream the sugar and butter in a mixer bowl until light and fluffy. Beat in the eggs.

▼ Dissolve the baking soda in the milk. Add to the creamed mixture and mix well. Add the bananas and vanilla and mix well. Mix the baking powder and flour together, add to the sugar mixture and mix well. Stir in the pecans. Pour into a greased 5x9-inch loaf pan.

▼ Bake at 325 degrees for 45 minutes or until the loaf tests done.

Yield: 12 slices

1 1/2 cups sugar
3/4 cup butter, softened
2 eggs
1 teaspoon baking soda
1/4 cup sour milk or buttermilk
1 cup mashed bananas
1 teaspoon vanilla extract
1 teaspoon baking powder
2 cups flour
1 cup chopped pecans

Miss Gayla's Pumpkin Bread

Although this is called pumpkin bread, it is reminiscent of gingerbread.

▼ Cream the shortening and sugar in a mixer bowl until light and fluffy. Beat in the eggs. Add the pumpkin and water and beat until well blended.

▼ Mix the flour, salt, baking powder, baking soda, cinnamon and cloves together. Add to the pumpkin mixture and mix until smooth.

▼ Stir in the molasses and raisins. Pour into 2 greased and floured 5x9-inch loaf pans or 5 greased and floured miniature loaf pans.

▼ Bake at 350 degrees for 40 minutes or until the loaves test done.

▼ Cool in the pans for several minutes. Invert onto wire racks to cool completely.

Yield: 24 slices

2/3 cup shortening or margarine
2 2/3 cups sugar
4 eggs
1 (16-ounce) can pumpkin
2/3 cup water
3 1/3 cups unsifted flour
1 1/2 teaspoons salt
1/2 teaspoon baking powder
2 teaspoons baking soda
1 teaspoon ground cinnamon
1 teaspoon ground cloves
3 to 4 tablespoons molasses
1 to 1 1/2 cups raisins

Spiced Zucchini Bread

3 cups flour
1 teaspoon salt
1¹/₂ teaspoons cinnamon
2 teaspoons baking soda
¹/₂ teaspoon baking powder
³/₄ cup chopped pecans
3 eggs
2 cups sugar
1 cup vegetable oil
2 teaspoons vanilla extract
2 cups shredded zucchini
1 (8-ounce) can crushed
   pineapple, drained

▼ Combine the flour, salt, cinnamon, baking soda and baking powder in a bowl and mix well. Stir in the pecans and set aside.

▼ Beat the eggs lightly in a large mixer bowl. Add the sugar, oil and vanilla and mix well.

▼ Add the zucchini and pineapple and stir until well mixed. Add the flour mixture and stir just until moistened. Spoon into 2 greased 5x9-inch loaf pans.

▼ Bake at 350 degrees for 1 hour or until the loaves test done.

▼ Cool in the pans for 10 minutes. Invert onto wire racks to cool completely.

Yield: 24 slices

Is There a Map?

The rumor persists that somewhere on the river-side of Amelia there lies about the largest gold hoard ever buried. It's somewhere near where the Amelia River meets the Nassau River and flows into the sea. Many expeditions have concentrated on that area, and without success.

Sunshine Muffins

▼ Mix the flour, sugar, baking powder, baking soda, salt and cinnamon in a large bowl. Add the apple, carrots, pecans, papaya, pineapple, apricots, raisins and coconut, mix well and set aside.

▼ Beat the eggs with the oil and vanilla in a small bowl. Add to the batter and mix well. Spoon into 12 greased muffin cups.

▼ Bake at 350 degrees for 25 minutes or until golden brown.

▼ May substitute one 6-ounce package of Mariani Tropical Medley found in the health food section of the grocery store for all fruit except the apple and use a large apple instead of a medium one.

Yield: 12 muffins

$1\frac{1}{4}$ **cups flour**
$1\frac{1}{4}$ **cups sugar**
$\frac{1}{2}$ **teaspoon baking powder**
$\frac{1}{2}$ **teaspoon baking soda**
$\frac{1}{4}$ **teaspoon salt**
$1\frac{1}{2}$ **teaspoons cinnamon**
1 medium apple, grated
$\frac{1}{2}$ **cup grated carrots**
$\frac{1}{2}$ **cup chopped pecans**
$\frac{1}{2}$ **cup chopped dried papaya**
$\frac{1}{2}$ **cup chopped dried pineapple**
$\frac{1}{2}$ **cup chopped dried apricots**
$\frac{1}{4}$ **cup raisins**
$\frac{1}{4}$ **cup shredded coconut**
2 eggs
$\frac{1}{2}$ **cup vegetable oil**
$1\frac{1}{2}$ **teaspoons vanilla extract**

Don't Spend It Yet!

The original map was on a piece of tattered canvas. A wavering line ran across the sheet from the upper right-hand corner to the lower left-hand corner. There was a dotted line, a compass bearing a large X, and these cryptic words: "Frm, Scarp, 3rd passage S.NNW to Nas 10 (degrees) by E fm 80-foot oak tree mkd old $\frac{1}{4}$ arp. tp lg bt."

Figure that out and start shoveling!

Swedish Oatmeal Pancakes

2 cups rolled oats
2 cups buttermilk
½ cup flour
3 tablespoons sugar
1 teaspoon baking powder
1 teaspoon baking soda
2 eggs, beaten
¼ cup melted butter

Serve these pancakes dusted with cinnamon-sugar or spread with honey. They are especially delicious when thin slices of apple or a few blueberries are added before baking.

▼ Combine the oats and buttermilk in a bowl and mix well. Let stand, covered, in the refrigerator for 8 to 10 hours.

▼ Sift the flour, sugar, baking powder and baking soda into the oat mixture. Add the eggs and melted butter and mix well.

▼ Pour the desired amount of batter onto a hot griddle. Bake until brown on both sides, turning once.

Yield: 16 pancakes

Beware Clanking Chains

One story that has recurred for generations is about a treasure marked by a chain hanging from a big oak tree. It seems a pirate had two men to row the boat in and dig the hole to bury his treasure, and the pirate hit them over the head with a big chain and covered them over with dirt atop his treasure. He swung the chain over the limb of the live oak to mark the spot and returned to his boat, on which he died. Several people are reported to have seen the chain hanging in the tree, but—by the time each goes home to get a shovel and comes back—tree, chain and treasure seem to vanish.

ℳany-Use Pizza Dough

This versatile dough will keep in the refrigerator for 3 or 4 days. Do not freeze the dough as it will toughen.

1 tablespoon dry yeast
1½ cups lukewarm water
2 tablespoons milk
¼ cup olive oil
1 teaspoon salt
4 cups flour

▼ Dissolve the yeast in the lukewarm water in a large bowl. Let stand for several minutes.

▼ Add the milk, olive oil, salt and flour and mix well with a wooden spoon or beat with an electric mixer fitted with dough hooks for 4 to 5 minutes.

▼ Turn onto a lightly floured surface and knead for 8 to 10 minutes. Place in an oiled bowl, turning to coat the surface.

▼ Let rise, tightly covered, in the refrigerator for 8 to 10 hours or, loosely covered, in a warm place for 1 hour or until doubled in bulk.

▼ Punch the dough down. Divide into portions. Pat to desired thickness on baking sheets, pizza pans or preheated baking stones to make 8 individual pizzas or 2 medium pizzas.

▼ Add pizza sauce and toppings as desired. Bake at 425 degrees for 8 to 10 minutes or until golden brown.

Yield: 8 servings

Variations: For *Calzones*, prepare dough as above and pat into circles of the desired size. Spread pizza sauce in the center and add toppings. Fold the edges over or toward the center and seal. Place on a baking sheet or baking stone. Bake for 10 minutes or until golden brown.

For *Focaccia*, dust a baking sheet with cornmeal. Pat the dough onto the baking sheet. "Dimple" the dough with your knuckles. Brush with olive oil and sprinkle with salt and your choice of herbs, such as rosemary or sage. Let rise, loosely covered with plastic wrap, for 15 to 20 minutes. Bake at 375 degrees for 10 to 15 minutes or until puffed and very lightly browned at the edges.

Mixin' & Minglin'

Salads

The Make-Up of Amelia

Amelia Island is indeed a natural wonder. Like most wonders, it didn't just happen, but rather is the result of an incredible interweaving of mineral, plant, and animal interdependence.

Let's begin at the bottom, with the earth. Hidden beneath our beaches and hammocks, below our marshes and estuaries, is a marvelous foundation of limestone. Over millions of years, as the seas converged and receded, this stone was formed by deposited layers of shells, silt, and sand.

But what of the sand? The fine white beaches we find along Amelia's Atlantic Coast are not limestone, but quartz. These sands have traveled slowly southward along the coast, washed by the sea from the eroding Appalachian Mountains, where they originated, to the beaches of Amelia Island, where they are deposited.

A limestone cake with an exposed icing of quartz and sand alone does not make Amelia Island. Our plants need nutrition to grow. This is the point at which the wondrous interdependency of nature becomes most apparent.

As the sea deposits the sands on our beaches, the east winds blow them inland, securely out of the water's reach. At the same time, particles of plantlife are deposited and, in turn, blown inland. The vegetation breaks down, adding nutrients to the soil until sturdy "pioneer" plants become established. Here the cycle of visible vegetation begins.

Continuing inland, the sand becomes more enriched by growing and dying plants until the vegetation becomes dense and variable enough to hold the soil and form a line of large sand dunes. These dunes support their own unique plants adapted to the salt winds, and also offer protection to the island's interior that allows a new variety of plantlife to thrive on the leeward side.

This new vegetation, with majestic oaks, a dense canopy of vine-laden limbs, and thick floor of palmettos, continues to the marshes on the westward side, where again only plants tolerant to salt may survive. From the marshes the sea obtains much of the plant matter necessary to continue the process of vegetating Amelia Island.

And so the cycle continues.

Champagne Salad

- ▼ Blend the cream cheese and sugar in a large bowl.
- ▼ Add the crushed pineapple and undrained strawberries and mix well.
- ▼ Fold in the banana slices and whipped topping.
- ▼ Spoon into a 9x13-inch dish, a loaf pan or a ring mold. Cover tightly.
- ▼ Freeze until firm. Cut into squares or unmold the loaf pan or ring mold onto a serving plate and slice into serving portions.
- ▼ Store any unused salad, tightly wrapped, in the freezer.

Yield: 8 servings

8 ounces cream cheese, softened
¾ cup sugar
1 (15-ounce) can crushed
  pineapple, drained
1 (10-ounce) package frozen
  strawberries, partially thawed
2 bananas, sliced
9 ounces whipped topping

Strawberry Pretzel Salad

- ▼ Combine the pretzels, margarine and ¼ cup sugar in a bowl and mix well.
- ▼ Press into a 9x13-inch baking dish. Bake at 400 degrees for 6 minutes. Cool completely.
- ▼ Combine the cream cheese, 1 cup sugar and whipped topping in a medium bowl. Beat until smooth and creamy. Spread over the cooled pretzel layer.
- ▼ Dissolve the gelatin in boiling water in a large bowl.
- ▼ Add the frozen strawberries and stir until the strawberries are thawed and the mixture is slightly thickened.
- ▼ Pour the strawberry mixture carefully over the cream cheese layer. Chill until firm.

Yield: 12 servings

2 cups crushed pretzels
¾ cup melted margarine
¼ cup sugar
8 ounces cream cheese, softened
1 cup sugar
12 ounces whipped topping
1 (6-ounce) package strawberry
  gelatin
2 cups boiling water
2 (10-ounce) packages frozen
  strawberries

Molded Cranberry Salad

1 (3-ounce) package blackberry
  gelatin
1 (3-ounce) package raspberry
  gelatin
2 cups boiling water
1 (16-ounce) can whole cranberry
  sauce
1 (20-ounce) can juice-pack
  crushed pineapple
1 cup chopped walnuts

▼ Dissolve the gelatins in boiling water in a large bowl.
▼ Add the cranberry sauce to the hot gelatin mixture and mix well.
▼ Drain the pineapple, reserving the juice. Add enough water to the reserved juice to measure ¾ cup. Add the pineapple and juice to the gelatin mixture. Add the walnuts. Pour the mixture into a large mold. Chill until firm.
▼ Unmold the gelatin onto a serving plate.

Yield: 10 to 12 servings

Florida Beef Salad

1 head leaf lettuce, torn
2 cucumbers, peeled
1 medium onion
1 green bell pepper
2 tomatoes
3 (16-ounce) cans small potatoes
1½ pounds cooked roast beef,
  sliced ¼ inch thick
1 (8-ounce) bottle Italian salad
  dressing
4 hard-cooked eggs, sliced
1 (4-ounce) can sliced black
  olives, drained
1 small jar capers, drained

▼ Line a large salad bowl with leaf lettuce.
▼ Slice the cucumbers and onion thinly. Cut the green pepper into halves and discard the seeds and membranes; slice thinly. Cut the tomatoes into wedges.
▼ Drain and slice the potatoes. (May substitute baked potatoes that have been peeled and sliced for canned.)
▼ Cut the roast beef into squares.
▼ Alternate layers of cucumbers, onion, green pepper, tomatoes, potatoes and roast beef in the salad bowl until all the ingredients are used. Pour the salad dressing over the layers.
▼ Arrange the egg slices over the top and sprinkle with the olives and capers.

Yield: 8 servings

Super Chicken Salad

▼ Combine the lime juice, garlic, ginger, parsley, mayonnaise and salt and pepper in a bowl, food processor or blender container and mix well. Store, covered, in the refrigerator.

▼ Rinse the chicken and pat dry. Bake or boil the chicken as desired, skin, bone and chop into bite-size pieces.

▼ Combine the chicken with the celery, green peppers, green onions and almonds in a large bowl.

▼ Add the desired amount of mayonnaise mixture and mix well. Chill until serving time. If the salad will not be served the same day, refrigerate the salad and dressing separately.

▼ Serve on salad plates or use as a spread on bread or crackers.

Yield: 4 to 6 servings

Variation: Make "shells" by pressing refrigerator biscuit or crescent roll dough into muffin cups or ramekins. Bake according to the package directions until golden brown, removing from the pans to cool. Spoon the chicken salad into the shells.

2 tablespoons lime juice
1 or 2 cloves of garlic, chopped
$1/2$ teaspoon ginger
$1/3$ bunch parsley, chopped
$1 1/2$ cups mayonnaise
Salt and pepper to taste
2 pounds chicken breasts
1 large rib celery, chopped
1 or 2 green bell peppers, chopped
1 bunch green onions, sliced
8 ounces almonds, chopped

Paella Salad

1 cup uncooked rice
1 teaspoon crushed saffron
2½ cups (about) chicken broth
½ cup (or more) Italian salad
   dressing with herbs
6 ounces smoked sausage
8 ounces shrimp, cooked, peeled
1 cup cubed cooked chicken
1 cup drained cooked peas
2 tomatoes, peeled, seeded,
   chopped
¼ cup chopped green bell pepper
¼ cup sliced green onions
Lettuce leaves
1 tomato, cut into wedges

▼ Mix the rice with saffron. Combine the rice mixture with the chicken broth in a medium saucepan. (Use the same amount of chicken broth as the water recommended in the package directions.)

▼ Bring to a boil, cover and reduce heat to a simmer. Simmer for 25 minutes.

▼ Combine the rice with ½ cup salad dressing in a large salad bowl and mix well.

▼ Refrigerate, covered, for 2 hours.

▼ Slice the sausage as desired. Cook, drain and set aside.

▼ Cut the shrimp into halves lengthwise and set aside.

▼ Add the peas, chopped tomatoes, green pepper and green onions to the rice mixture and mix gently.

▼ Fold in the sausage, shrimp and chicken. Add additional salad dressing if necessary to moisten.

▼ Refrigerate, covered, until ready to serve.

▼ Line the the salad plates with lettuce. Spoon the salad onto the prepared plates.

▼ Arrange tomato wedges on each plate.

Yield: 6 servings

Ham and Bleu Cheese Pasta Salad

This special recipe comes from the Biltmore House in Asheville, North Carolina.

▼ Cook the pasta according to the package directions. Drain, rinse with cold water and drain well.

▼ Combine the pasta with the ham, pecans, bleu cheese and parsley in a large bowl.

▼ Mix the rosemary and garlic with the olive oil and add to the pasta mixture.

▼ Add the Parmesan cheese and toss to mix.

▼ Chill, covered, until serving time.

Yield: 4 servings

4 cups bowtie pasta
6 ounces cooked ham, cut into $\frac{1}{4}$-inch strips
1 cup chopped pecans
5 ounces bleu cheese, crumbled
$\frac{1}{2}$ cup chopped parsley
2 tablespoons minced rosemary
1 clove of garlic, minced
$\frac{1}{3}$ cup olive oil
$\frac{1}{3}$ cup freshly grated Parmesan cheese

American Beach

In 1935, A. L. Lewis, Florida's first black millionaire, founded American Beach as a place where people of color could enjoy ocean beaches during the days of segregation. Mr. Lewis was the founder of the Afro-American Life Insurance Company, the first insurance company—black or white—in the state of Florida. During its heyday, American Beach played host to as many as ten thousand people on a weekend. It was the only Florida beach where blacks were allowed to spend the night. American Beach's Beach Motel is the oldest oceanfront black-owned motel in the United States. Then and now American Beach lays claim to many famous residents: Mama Williams, one of the founders of the Urban League; Dr. Harry Richardson, the first black man to graduate from Harvard University's Theological Seminary; and Leander J. Shaw, Jr., the first black judge to become Chief Justice of the State Supreme Court for a two-year term (1990–92)—just to name a few.

Portable Pasta Salad

1 cup sour cream
1 (4-ounce) can chopped green
   chiles
1 teaspoon ground cumin
   (optional)
9 lasagna noodles, cooked,
   drained
1 (12-ounce) can Mexican-style
   corn, drained
4 cups shredded lettuce
1 (16-ounce) jar salsa
12 hard-cooked eggs, sliced
1 cup shredded Monterey Jack
   cheese

▼ Combine the sour cream, green chiles and cumin in a small bowl and mix well.

▼ Arrange 3 of the noodles in the bottom of a 9x13-inch dish.

▼ Add layers of ½ cup corn, 1⅓ cups lettuce, ¾ cup salsa, slices of 5 eggs and ⅓ cup shredded cheese.

▼ Repeat the layers, beginning with the noodles but substituting the sour cream mixture for the salsa layer.

▼ Repeat the layers with the remaining noodles, remaining corn, remaining lettuce, ¾ cup salsa, remaining eggs and remaining cheese.

▼ Spoon the remaining salsa over the top. Cover tightly.

▼ Chill until serving time.

▼ Cut the salad into squares to serve a portion of all the layers.

Yield: 12 servings

Variation: Instead of canned Mexican-style corn, substitute 1½ cups cooked and drained fresh corn (about 3 ears) mixed with 2 tablespoons each chopped green and red bell pepper.

Broccoli Salad

▼ Chop the broccoli as desired. Combine with the onion in a large bowl.

▼ Add the cheese and bacon and toss to mix.

▼ Blend the mayonnaise with sugar and vinegar in a small bowl.

▼ Add to the broccoli mixture and toss to mix.

▼ Refrigerate, covered, overnight.

Yield: 8 servings

1 bunch fresh broccoli
1/2 onion, finely chopped
8 ounces shredded Cheddar cheese
8 ounces bacon, crisp-cooked, crumbled
1 cup mayonnaise
1/2 cup sugar
2 tablespoons vinegar

Marinated Slaw

▼ Cut up the cabbage, green pepper and onion as desired for slaw. Combine the vegetables in a large bowl and toss to mix.

▼ Combine the sugar, vinegar, oil, dry mustard, celery seeds and salt in a saucepan and mix well.

▼ Bring the mixture to a boil over medium heat, stirring until the sugar dissolves. Reduce the heat and simmer for 2 to 3 minutes. Let stand until cool.

▼ Pour the mixture over the vegetables and mix well.

▼ Refrigerate, covered, for 24 hours before serving.

Yield: 8 to 10 servings

1 medium head cabbage
1 green bell pepper
1 onion
3/4 cup sugar
3/4 cup vinegar
1/2 cup vegetable oil
1 teaspoon dry mustard
1 teaspoon celery seeds
1 teaspoon salt

Caesar Salad

1 large head romaine
2 cloves of garlic, pressed
6 tablespoons olive oil
1 tablespoon wine vinegar
1 tablespoon German mustard
1½ teaspoons steak sauce
1½ teaspoons Worcestershire
  sauce
2 teaspoons lemon juice
1 egg
⅛ teaspoon each thyme and
  oregano
Salt and pepper to taste
½ cup grated Parmesan cheese
1 ounce anchovies
1 cup croutons

▼ Rinse the romaine and pat the leaves dry. Tear the leaves into large pieces and place in a salad bowl.
▼ Combine the garlic, olive oil, wine vinegar, mustard, steak sauce, Worcestershire sauce and lemon juice in a small bowl and whisk until well mixed.
▼ Add the egg, thyme, oregano, salt and pepper and whisk until well mixed.
▼ Pour the dressing over the romaine and toss until coated.
▼ Top with the Parmesan cheese, anchovies and croutons.

Yield: 4 servings

Wilted Greens with Bacon Dressing

½ cup fresh green peas
2 cups boiling water
6 cups gourmet salad greens
½ cup thinly sliced green onions
4 slices bacon, chopped
¼ cup water
2 tablespoons red wine vinegar
2 tablespoons fresh lemon juice
Coarsely ground pepper to taste

▼ Cook the peas in 2 cups boiling water for 7 minutes or until tender-crisp. Drain, rinse with cold water and drain well.
▼ Combine the peas, greens and green onions in a salad bowl and set aside.
▼ Cook the bacon in a skillet until crisp. Add ¼ cup water, vinegar and lemon juice. Cook for 2 minutes.
▼ Pour the hot dressing over the salad and toss gently.
▼ Sprinkle with pepper and serve immediately.

Yield: 4 servings

ℳixed 𝒢reen 𝒮alad

▼ Combine the garlic and olive oil in a small bowl. Let stand for 2 hours.

▼ Cut the tomatoes into pieces and chop the green onions. Combine the tomatoes, green onions and parsley in a large salad bowl. Add the garlic oil.

▼ Sprinkle with thyme or basil and salt and toss to mix. Let stand for 30 minutes.

▼ Add the salad greens and toss to mix well.

▼ Sprinkle with the lemon juice, feta cheese and pepper.

▼ Toss again and serve immediately.

Yield: 4 servings

1 clove of garlic, minced
6 tablespoons olive oil
2 tomatoes
3 green onions
1/3 cup minced parsley
3/4 teaspoon dried thyme or basil, crushed
1/2 teaspoon salt
4 servings torn mixed salad greens such as romaine, green and red leaf and Boston lettuce
1 1/2 to 2 tablespoons lemon juice
4 ounces feta cheese, crumbled
Freshly ground pepper to taste

ℛomaine with ℰndive and ℬean 𝒮alad

▼ Combine the water, vinegar, oregano, pepper and garlic in a small bowl and whisk until blended.

▼ Add the beans, toss until coated and set aside.

▼ Layer the romaine and endive on salad plates. Spoon mounds of the bean mixture on the prepared plates.

▼ Sprinkle with the Parmesan cheese and serve immediately.

Yield: 6 servings

1/4 cup water
2 1/2 tablespoons red wine vinegar
1/2 teaspoon dried oregano
1/4 teaspoon pepper
1 clove of garlic, crushed
1 (16-ounce) can navy beans, drained
6 cups torn romaine
Leaves of 2 heads Belgian endive
1/4 cup freshly grated Parmesan cheese

Shakespeare's Kitchen House Salad

1/2 cup pecans
8 ounces mixed organic field
   greens
1 Granny Smith apple, diced
4 ounces bleu cheese, crumbled
Raspberry Vinaigrette

Shakespeare's Kitchen, located in beautiful, historic downtown Fernandina Beach, shared this special recipe with us. We know you'll love it.

▼ Sprinkle the pecans evenly on a baking sheet. Bake at 350 degrees for 3 to 5 minutes or until lightly toasted, stirring once or twice. Let stand until cool.

▼ Combine the greens, apple, bleu cheese and toasted pecans in a large salad bowl.

▼ Add the desired amount of Raspberry Vinaigrette and toss to mix.

▼ Serve immediately.

Raspberry Vinaigrette

1 cup olive oil
1/2 cup red wine vinegar
1/4 cup water
1/4 cup vegetable oil
1 teaspoon freshly cracked pepper
2 tablespoons sugar
1 cup raspberries

▼ Combine the olive oil, vinegar, water, vegetable oil, pepper, sugar and raspberries in a food processor container.

▼ Pulse several times to blend well. Pour into a bowl or bottle.

▼ Store, covered, in the refrigerator.

Yield: 4 servings

Apple and Pecan Spinach Salad

▼ Rinse the spinach well. Discard stems and pat dry.
▼ Combine the spinach, onion, pecans and apple in a salad bowl and toss to mix.
▼ Combine the olive oil, lemon juice, sugar, garlic and salt in a small bowl and whisk until well blended.
▼ Pour the dressing over the spinach mixture and toss to coat.
▼ Serve immediately.

Yield: 8 servings

10 ounces fresh spinach
1 cup thinly sliced red onion
1 cup chopped pecans
1 Granny Smith apple, thinly sliced
1/2 cup olive oil
3 tablespoons lemon juice
2 tablespoons sugar
1 clove of garlic, crushed
1 teaspoon salt

Spinach Salad with Black Beans

▼ Combine the spinach, beans, mushrooms, red pepper, onion and bacon in a salad bowl and set aside.
▼ Combine the picante sauce, salad dressing and cumin in a small bowl and whisk until well mixed.
▼ Pour the dressing over the spinach mixture and toss lightly.
▼ Cut the eggs into slices or wedges and arrange over the salad.

Yield: 4 servings

4 cups torn spinach leaves
1 (15-ounce) can black beans, rinsed, drained
1 cup sliced mushrooms
1 red bell pepper, cut into strips
1/2 cup thinly sliced red onion rings
1/4 cup julienne Canadian bacon
1/2 cup picante sauce
1/4 cup Italian salad dressing
1/4 teaspoon ground cumin
2 hard-cooked eggs

Hot Potato Salad

6 medium potatoes
2 hard-cooked eggs, chopped
4 slices bacon, chopped
¼ cup finely chopped onion
1 egg, beaten
¼ cup vinegar
¼ cup water
1 teaspoon salt
1 teaspoon sugar
¼ teaspoon pepper

▼ Cook the potatoes as desired, peel and slice. Combine the potato slices and hard-cooked eggs in a large bowl. Set aside.

▼ Fry the bacon and chopped onion in a skillet until light brown. Strain, reserving the bacon drippings. Add the bacon and onion to the potato mixture and toss lightly.

▼ Add the reserved bacon drippings to the beaten egg gradually, beating constantly.

▼ Add the vinegar, water, salt, sugar and pepper to the egg mixture, beating constantly until well blended.

▼ Pour the mixture over the potato mixture and toss until well mixed.

▼ Serve immediately.

Yield: 6 servings

Ricotta Potato Salad

3 pounds red or new white
  potatoes
Salt to taste
⅔ cup freshly grated Parmesan
  cheese
1 cup ricotta cheese
4 cloves of garlic, pressed
½ red onion, very thinly sliced
½ cup olive oil
6 tablespoons cider vinegar
Pepper to taste
½ cup chopped fresh parsley

▼ Peel the potatoes and cut into cubes. There should be about 12 cups of the potato cubes. Cook in boiling salted water to cover in a large saucepan just until tender.

▼ Drain well and place in a large bowl.

▼ Add the Parmesan cheese, ricotta cheese, garlic, onion, olive oil, vinegar, salt and pepper to the hot potatoes and toss until well mixed.

▼ Mix in the parsley.

▼ Refrigerate, covered, until serving time.

Yield: 8 servings

Marinated Vegetable Salad

▼ Drain the canned vegetables well. Combine the canned vegetables with the celery and onion in a large bowl.

▼ Add the Marinade and mix well.

▼ Refrigerate, covered, for several hours before serving. This salad will keep in the refrigerator for up to 2 weeks.

1 (16-ounce) can French-style green beans
1 (16-ounce) can green peas
1 (16-ounce) can Shoepeg corn
1 (2-ounce) jar chopped pimento
1 cup chopped celery
1 cup chopped onion
Marinade (below)

Marinade

▼ Combine the vinegar, oil, sugar, water, salt and pepper in a saucepan.

▼ Bring to a boil, stirring until the sugar dissolves. Let stand until cool.

Yield: 6 to 8 servings

3/4 cup vinegar
1/2 cup vegetable oil
1 cup sugar
1 tablespoon water
1 teaspoon each salt and pepper

Where It All Started

Seafood

Shrimping

Fernandina Beach is recognized as the birthplace of the modern shrimping industry. In the early part of this century technological advances that occurred in the waters around Amelia Island transformed shrimping into an offshore, deep-water activity in which motorized trawlers took the place of rowboats and sailboats.

The evolution of modern shrimping began in 1902 when Mike Salvador, a Sicilian immigrant, was the first to go into deeper water pulling a haul seine from his power boat. In 1913, Captain Billy Corkum adapted the otter trawl, a bag-like net that had weighted doors, which is still seen on shrimp boats today. Captain William Jones Davis, a local bar pilot, was the first to use a power boat to drag the trawl net. In 1922, David Cook and Emmett Freeman added corners and wings for better operation, thus adding to the refinement of the trawl net.

As technology improved, shrimp boats moved further offshore in search of larger varieties of shrimp. Local shrimper Harry Sahlman is credited with pioneering the expansion of the shrimping grounds in the 1940s to the deeper waters of Central and South America, where he developed ways to catch Royal Red shrimp in the two-hundred-fathom-deep waters of Campeche, Mexico.

Fish Poached in White Wine

▼ Sprinkle the fish with the sea salt and pepper.

▼ Mix the wine and lemon juice in a pan suitable for poaching. If the pan is large, add enough additional poaching liquid to come halfway up the fish. Bring the wine mixture to a simmer.

▼ Place the fish in the simmering liquid. Place the tarragon in the liquid and sprinkle the chives over the fish with a bit in the poaching liquid.

▼ Cover the pan. Simmer very gently for 4 minutes for thin flounder fillets to 6 minutes for thicker haddock fillets, or until the fish flakes easily. Remove from the poaching liquid carefully and serve immediately.

Yield: 2 servings

8 ounces white-fleshed fish fillets such as flounder or halibut
1/8 teaspoon sea salt
1/8 teaspoon pepper
1/4 cup dry white wine
1 tablespoon lemon juice
1 (2-inch) sprig of fresh tarragon
1 tablespoon minced fresh chives

Parmesan Basil Fish

▼ Combine the lemon and olive oil in a blender container and process until puréed.

▼ Preheat a large skillet over medium-high heat. Add the olive oil mixture. Cook for 1 minute.

▼ Add the garlic and basil. Sauté for several minutes.

▼ Add the bread crumbs and mix until well coated with the olive oil mixture.

▼ Sauté until the crumbs are dry. Pour the crumbs into a bowl. Mix in the Parmesan cheese and pepper.

▼ Arrange the fish fillets in an oiled baking pan. Spoon the crumb mixture over the fillets.

▼ Bake, covered, at 350 degrees for 20 minutes or until the fish flakes easily with a fork.

Yield: 4 servings

1/2 lemon, peeled, seeded
1/2 cup olive oil
2 large cloves of garlic, minced
3 tablespoons fresh basil, or 1 tablespoon dried
2 cups bread crumbs
2/3 cup freshly grated Parmesan cheese
1/8 teaspoon pepper
2 pounds fish fillets

Grilled Mahimahi with Tropical Fruit Salsa

1/3 cup extra-virgin olive oil
Grated zest of 1 lime
1 tablespoon chopped fresh
 cilantro or parsley
2 tablespoons cracked black
 pepper
4 (6-ounce) mahimahi (dolphin
 fish) fillets
1 teaspoon salt
Tropical Fruit Salsa

*If you like "Innovative Island Cuisine with a Tropical Flair"
try this creative recipe from Cafe Atlantis, located in the
heart of Historic Fernandina Beach.*

▼ Combine the olive oil, lime zest, cilantro and pepper in a
small bowl and mix well.
▼ Rub the mixture over the fillets, coating well. Refrigerate
while preparing the salsa.
▼ Sprinkle with the salt just before grilling.
▼ Grill the fillets for 3 to 4 minutes on each side or just
until the fish is opaque.
▼ Serve immediately with a large spoonful of the Tropical
Fruit Salsa. Garnish with cilantro sprigs.
▼ May substitute bluefish, swordfish or other firm, fatty fish
for mahimahi.

Tropical Fruit Salsa

1 mango or 2 or 3 fresh peaches
1/2 fresh pineapple
1 red bell pepper
1 habañero or jalapeño pepper
Juice of 1 lime
1 tablespoon chopped fresh
 cilantro
1 teaspoon sugar
1/2 teaspoon salt

▼ Peel and section the mango. Core and peel the
pineapple. Cut the mango and pineapple in small dice.
▼ Dice the red pepper into slightly smaller pieces than the
mango and pineapple.
▼ Seed, devein and finely chop the habañero pepper.
(Protect your hands with rubber gloves and do not get
the juice in your eyes.)
▼ Combine the mango, pineapple, peppers, lime juice,
cilantro, sugar and salt in a medium bowl and mix well.
▼ Let stand for about 30 minutes to allow flavors to marry.
▼ Adjust the sugar and salt before serving.

Yield: 4 servings

Trout Amandine

Just about any mild fish works well with this recipe.

2 pounds trout fillets
1/4 cup flour
1 teaspoon seasoned salt
1 teaspoon paprika
2 tablespoons melted butter
1/2 cup sliced almonds
2 tablespoons butter
2 tablespoons lemon juice
1 tablespoon chopped parsley

▼ Cut the fillets into 6 portions.

▼ Mix the flour, seasoned salt and paprika in a shallow dish.

▼ Coat the fillets with the flour mixture and arrange skin side down in a single layer in a well greased baking or broiler pan.

▼ Drizzle 2 tablespoons melted butter over the fillets.

▼ Broil about 4 inches from the heat source for 5 to 10 minutes or just until the fish flakes easily when tested with a fork.

▼ Sauté the almonds in the remaining 2 tablespoons butter in a small skillet until golden brown. Remove from the heat and mix in the lemon juice and parsley.

▼ Place the fillets on serving plates and spoon the almonds over the top. Serve immediately.

Yield: 6 servings

Sesame Seared Tuna with Cucumber Sambal

4 (8-ounce) yellowfin tuna steaks
¾ cup black sesame seeds
1 tablespoon vegetable oil
Cucumber Sambal

Fine dining at the Beech Street Grill, located in the historic district, is always a delight. This recipe will be one of your favorites.

▼ Preheat a large sauté pan over high heat.
▼ Coat the tuna on all sides with the sesame seeds.
▼ Add the oil to the hot pan. Place the tuna in the pan. Cook for 1 to 2 minutes on each side for rare (the recommended degree of doneness).
▼ Mound the Cucumber Sambal in the center of the plates. Slice the tuna and arrange in a fan pattern around the sambal.
▼ Serve with soy sauce or a very hot mustard.

Cucumber Sambal

2 cucumbers
½ large carrot, peeled, grated
½ red onion, finely chopped
1 tablespoon hot red pepper flakes
½ cup white vinegar
2 tablespoons sugar
1 tablespoon each chopped fresh cilantro, mint and basil
Salt and black pepper to taste

▼ Cut the cucumbers into halves lengthwise and slice thinly.
▼ Combine the cucumber slices with the carrot, onion, red pepper flakes, vinegar, sugar, cilantro, mint, basil, salt and black pepper in a medium bowl and mix well. The sambal may be made ahead and refrigerated, covered, for 1 to 2 days.

Yield: 4 servings

Crab Cakes with Dijon Dressing

- ▼ Combine the crab meat, bread crumbs, egg white, mayonnaise, parsley, mustard, celery salt, pepper and salt in a large bowl and mix well.
- ▼ Shape into 6 patties and place on a plate.
- ▼ Chill, covered, for 1 hour.
- ▼ Heat the oil in a large nonstick skillet over medium heat.
- ▼ Arrange the crab cakes in the skillet. Cook for 3 minutes on each side or until golden brown. Drain on paper towels.
- ▼ Serve the crab cakes hot or chill if desired.
- ▼ Place 2 patties on each plate. Top with Dijon Dressing and garnish with lemon slices.

    Yield: 3 servings

1 pound fresh lump crab meat, drained, flaked
$2/3$ cup soft bread crumbs
1 egg white, lightly beaten
2 tablespoons mayonnaise
1 tablespoon chopped fresh parsley
$1/2$ teaspoon prepared mustard
$1/4$ teaspoon celery salt
$1/4$ teaspoon freshly ground pepper
$1/8$ teaspoon salt
1 tablespoon vegetable oil
Dijon Dressing

Dijon Dressing

- ▼ Combine the mayonnaise, mustard and Worcestershire sauce in a bowl and blend well.
- ▼ Refrigerate, covered, until ready to serve.
- ▼ Store any unused dressing in a tightly covered container in the refrigerator.

    Yield: 6 servings

1 cup mayonnaise
$1/4$ cup Dijon mustard
1 teaspoon Worcestershire sauce

Crab Fettuccini with Basil Cream Sauce

3 tablespoons butter
3 tablespoons olive oil
4 plum tomatoes, peeled, sliced
1 clove of garlic, finely chopped
1/3 to 1/2 cup dry white wine
1/3 cup cream
1 pound fresh fettuccini
Salt to taste
1/2 cup finely chopped fresh basil
2 cups cooked backfin crab meat
Pepper to taste
1/4 cup chopped fresh parsley
**1/4 cup freshly grated Parmesan
  cheese**

*Serve this wonderful pasta with a salad, crusty French bread
and wine. You can substitute lobster or shrimp.*

▼ Heat the butter and olive oil in a large heavy saucepan
  over medium heat.

▼ Add the tomatoes and garlic. Cook over low heat until
  the tomatoes are soft and beginning to cook down.

▼ Add 1/3 cup white wine and the cream. Simmer for 10
  minutes, adding a small amount of additional wine if the
  mixture becomes thicker than the consistency of heavy
  cream.

▼ Cook the pasta in boiling salted water until al dente
  while the sauce is simmering. Drain the pasta well.

▼ Add the basil, crab meat, salt and pepper to the sauce,
  stirring to mix well. Simmer for 3 minutes or until heated
  to serving temperature.

▼ Add half the parsley and half the Parmesan cheese and
  mix well.

▼ Add the hot pasta and toss to mix.

▼ Place the pasta on a serving platter. Sprinkle with the
  remaining parsley and Parmesan cheese.

Yield: 6 to 8 servings

Oyster and Eggplant Gratin

▼ Peel the eggplant and cut into ½-inch cubes. Finely chop the onion and red peppers. Cut the mushrooms into thin slices.

▼ Heat the olive oil in a large skillet over medium heat.

▼ Add the vegetables. Stir-fry for 3 to 5 minutes or until the vegetables are tender-crisp. Remove from the heat.

▼ Add the basil, oregano, parsley and oysters. Mix well and set aside.

▼ Spray a shallow 3-quart baking dish with nonstick cooking spray.

▼ Spread 1½ cups of the stuffing mix in the baking dish.

▼ Layer with half the vegetable mixture and half the cheese.

▼ Add layers of 1½ cups stuffing mix, remaining vegetable mixture and remaining cheese.

▼ Combine the chicken broth, hot pepper sauce, salt and pepper in a medium bowl and whisk until blended. Pour over the layers.

▼ Sprinkle the remaining stuffing mix on top.

▼ Bake in the middle of the oven at 375 degrees for 45 to 50 minutes or until golden brown and bubbly. Do not overbake or the oysters will be tough.

Yield: 6 to 8 servings

1 medium eggplant
1 medium onion
2 red bell peppers
8 ounces fresh mushrooms
¼ cup olive oil
⅓ cup finely chopped fresh basil
Oregano to taste
2 tablespoons finely chopped
   fresh parsley
2 pounds freshly shucked oysters,
   drained
4 cups herb-seasoned stuffing mix
3 cups shredded Gruyère cheese
1½ cups chicken broth
1 teaspoon hot pepper sauce
Salt and pepper to taste

Oysters Piquante

36 medium to large oysters
1 cup mayonnaise
2 tablespoons chili sauce
1 tablespoon melted butter
1¹/₂ teaspoons prepared mustard
1 teaspoon lemon juice
3 to 5 dashes of Tabasco sauce
¹/₄ teaspoon salt or seasoned salt
Pepper to taste
¹/₈ teaspoon paprika
1 cup soft bread crumbs or
   cracker crumbs

Serve this tangy, tasty dish as an appetizer or a fish course for dinner. Adjust the spicy ingredients to make the recipe hotter or milder for your taste preference.

▼ Prepare 12 baking shells or ramekins. Shuck, rinse and drain the oysters.

▼ Place 3 oysters in each baking shell. Place the shells on a baking sheet.

▼ Combine the mayonnaise, chili sauce, butter, mustard, lemon juice, Tabasco sauce, salt, pepper and paprika in a bowl and blend well.

▼ Spoon the mayonnaise mixture evenly over the oysters.

▼ Top with the bread or cracker crumbs.

▼ Broil about 3 inches from the heat source for 3 to 5 minutes or just until the oysters begin to curl at the edges and the crumbs are golden brown. Do not overcook or the oysters will be tough.

Yield: 12 servings

Scallops au Gratin

▼ Cut the scallops into fourths.

▼ Combine the wine and water in a large nonstick skillet over high heat. Bring to a boil.

▼ Add the scallops and reduce the heat to very low. Poach, covered, for 3 to 5 minutes or just until the scallops are firm and cooked through. Drain, reserving the cooking liquid and removing the scallops to a bowl.

▼ Melt the margarine in the skillet over medium-low heat. Add the onion and garlic. Sauté until tender.

▼ Add the flour. Cook for 1 minute, stirring constantly.

▼ Stir in the reserved cooking liquid. Cook for 3 to 5 minutes or until thickened, stirring constantly. Remove from the heat and cool slightly.

▼ Add the egg and parsley gradually, whisking until well blended. Add the salt and pepper.

▼ Add the scallops, folding in gently.

▼ Spoon the mixture into a shallow 4-cup baking dish or 4 ramekins.

▼ Sprinkle evenly with the Parmesan cheese.

▼ Broil 4 inches from the heat source for 3 to 4 minutes or until bubbly and golden brown.

Yield: 4 servings

1 1/4 **pounds trimmed sea scallops**
1/4 **cup dry white wine**
1/4 **cup water**
4 **teaspoons margarine**
1 **cup chopped onion**
1 **clove of garlic, minced**
4 **teaspoons flour**
1 **egg, beaten**
1 **tablespoon chopped parsley**
1/4 **teaspoon salt**
1/4 **teaspoon freshly ground pepper**
3/4 **ounce Parmesan cheese, freshly grated**

Shrimp Creole

1 medium onion, chopped
1 green bell pepper, chopped
1/2 cup sliced fresh mushrooms
2 tablespoons butter
1 (16-ounce) can stewed tomatoes
1 (16-ounce) can tomato sauce
1 (16-ounce) can tomato paste
1/2 teaspoon Creole seasonings
1 1/2 teaspoons sugar
1/8 teaspoon paprika
2 bay leaves
1 1/2 pounds large shrimp, peeled, deveined
4 servings hot cooked rice

▼ Sauté the onion, green pepper and mushrooms in the butter in a large skillet until tender.

▼ Add the tomatoes, tomato sauce, tomato paste, Creole seasonings, sugar, paprika and bay leaves, mixing well. Bring to a boil. Reduce the heat.

▼ Simmer, uncovered, for 20 minutes, stirring occasionally.

▼ Add the shrimp. Simmer for 10 to 20 minutes or until the shrimp turn pink, stirring occasionally.

▼ Remove and discard the bay leaves.

▼ Serve the Shrimp Creole over the rice. Garnish with lemon wedges.

Yield: 4 servings

Flowing Ocean Furrows

When new types of nets and boats started making their impact on Fernandina's burgeoning shrimping industry in the early part of this century, there was an immediate need for boat motors to enable the shrimpers to move further offshore to untapped shrimp grounds. But whereas men could build boats and sew nets, finding or manufacturing motors was an entirely different kettle of fish—or shrimp. In the race to make their fortunes, some of the early shrimpers had to rely on wit and ingenuity to power their trawlers.

One of the early automobile dealerships on Amelia Island was also saddled with the job of selling tractors. While cars were slowly catching on, the dealership could never meet its quota of tractor sales. That all changed when some enterprising shrimper discovered that you could power a shrimp boat with a tractor motor! Suddenly, tractors were selling—even though they didn't appear in the fields. Some people speculate that somewhere on Amelia Island there is a big tractor graveyard—and that not a one of those tractor carcasses houses a motor!

Island Shrimp Gumbo

This is a very old Florida recipe—tried and true, easy and soooo good!

▼ Chop the bacon into pieces. Chop the green pepper and onion.

▼ Fry the bacon in a large skillet until crisp. Remove the bacon from the drippings, drain on paper towels and set aside.

▼ Sauté the green pepper and onion in the bacon drippings until tender.

▼ Process the tomatoes in a blender until finely chopped. Pour into the skillet.

▼ Sprinkle with the flour, salt and pepper and mix well.

▼ Stir in the okra and bacon.

▼ Simmer for 20 minutes or until the okra is tender, stirring occasionally.

▼ Add the shrimp. Simmer for 5 minutes or until the shrimp turn pink.

▼ Serve over the rice.

Yield: 4 servings

3 slices bacon
1 green bell pepper
1 onion
2 (16-ounce) cans tomatoes
2 tablespoons flour
1 teaspoon salt
$1/4$ teaspoon pepper
2 cups sliced okra
1 pound shrimp, peeled, deveined
Hot cooked rice

Shrimp and Chicken Curry

1½ cups instant rice
3 chicken breasts, boned, cut up
1 pound shrimp, peeled, deveined
1 teaspoon butter
¼ teaspoon salt
1 teaspoon pepper
2 teaspoons curry powder
2 teaspoons garlic powder
1 teaspoon lemon juice
Dash of Tabasco sauce
1 (10-ounce) can cream of
   chicken soup
¼ cup milk
1 cup shredded sharp Cheddar
   cheese
2 cups croutons

A favorite among locals and tourists, the Marina Restaurant, located on Centre Street for fifty-five years, has graciously donated this fabulous recipe.

▼ Cook the rice according to the package directions and set aside.
▼ Rinse the chicken and pat dry.
▼ Sauté the chicken and shrimp in the butter in a large skillet until tender.
▼ Add the salt, pepper, curry powder, garlic powder, lemon juice and Tabasco sauce and mix well.
▼ Mix the soup and milk together. Stir into the skillet. Simmer over low heat for several minutes.
▼ Spread the rice evenly in a 2-quart baking dish sprayed with nonstick cooking spray.
▼ Remove the chicken and shrimp from the skillet with a slotted spoon and arrange over the rice.
▼ Pour the soup mixture over the chicken and shrimp.
▼ Bake at 375 degrees for 10 to 12 minutes.
▼ Top with the cheese and croutons. Bake for 3 to 5 minutes longer or until the cheese melts and the croutons are golden brown.
▼ Serve the curry with a tossed salad, French bread and red wine.

Yield: 6 servings

Fried Shrimp

These shrimp are like the shrimp served at O'Steen's Restaurant in St. Augustine. Great!

5 pounds large shrimp
2 pounds cracker meal
Salt and pepper to taste
6 eggs
½ gallon milk
1 gallon vegetable oil for deep-frying

▼ Peel the shrimp, leaving the tails on. Butterfly the shrimp by cutting halfway through from the head to about three-fourths of the way toward the tail.

▼ Mix the cracker meal with salt and pepper in a bowl and set aside.

▼ Beat the eggs in a large bowl. Add the milk and beat until well blended.

▼ Heat the oil in a deep fryer or large skillet.

▼ Dip the shrimp in the egg mixture and roll in the cracker meal until well coated.

▼ Place the shrimp in the hot oil. Fry until golden brown. Do not overcook. Drain well on paper towels.

Yield: 10 servings

Variation: For a sweeter taste, peel and butterfly the shrimp as above. Omit the egg mixture and cracker meal and prepare 2 packages of light pancake mix according to the package directions, dipping the shrimp into the prepared batter. Deep-fry until golden brown.

Sautéed Shrimp with Cheese Grits

1 cup chopped bacon
½ cup sliced green bell pepper
½ cup sliced red bell pepper
1 pound medium shrimp, peeled,
  deveined
2 teaspoons hot pepper sauce
Cheese Grits

▼ Cook the bacon in a large skillet until crisp. Drain the bacon, reserving 2 tablespoons bacon drippings.
▼ Sauté the green and red peppers in the reserved bacon drippings in the skillet until tender. Remove the peppers and set aside.
▼ Sauté the shrimp in the skillet until the shrimp turn pink.
▼ Return the sautéed peppers to the skillet. Add the hot pepper sauce.
▼ Serve the shrimp mixture over the Cheese Grits. Sprinkle with the crisp bacon.

Cheese Grits

1½ cups chicken broth
1½ cups milk
¾ cup quick-cooking grits
¼ teaspoon salt
1 cup shredded Cheddar cheese

▼ Bring the broth and milk to a boil in a large saucepan.
▼ Stir in the grits and salt. Cover and reduce the heat.
▼ Cook for 5 minutes, stirring occasionally.
▼ Stir in the cheese until melted. Set aside and keep warm.

Yield: 4 servings

*M*arinated *S*hrimp and *O*ranges

▼ Bring a large pot of water to a boil. Add the shrimp. Cook for 2 minutes or until the shrimp turn pink.

▼ Drain the shrimp and rinse with cold water until completely cooled. Drain well.

▼ Combine the shrimp, orange sections and onion slices in a large bowl.

▼ Combine the vinegar, oil, lemon juice, ketchup, sugar, capers, parsley, salt, mustard seeds, celery seeds, pepper and garlic in a medium bowl and mix well.

▼ Add to the shrimp mixture and mix gently.

▼ Refrigerate, covered, for 8 to 10 hours, stirring occasionally.

▼ Serve the shrimp mixture on a bed of shredded lettuce.

Yield: 12 servings

3 pounds large shrimp, peeled, deveined
4 oranges, peeled, sectioned
4 medium white onions, sliced
1¹/₂ cups cider vinegar
1 cup vegetable oil
²/₃ cup fresh lemon juice
¹/₂ cup ketchup
¹/₄ cup sugar
2 tablespoons drained capers
2 tablespoons minced parsley
2 teaspoons salt
2 teaspoons mustard seeds
1 teaspoon celery seeds
¹/₄ teaspoon pepper
2 cloves of garlic, crushed
Shredded lettuce

Asparagus and Shrimp Penne

²/₃ **cup dry white wine**
¹/₄ **teaspoon saffron threads**
2 pounds fresh asparagus
Salt to taste
2 tablespoons olive oil
1 pound shrimp, peeled, deveined
1 pound penne
¹/₄ **cup minced shallots**
1¹/₂ cups whipping cream
³/₄ **cup canned chicken broth**
Pepper to taste
¹/₄ **cup minced chives**

▼ Combine the wine and saffron in a small bowl. Let stand for 20 minutes.

▼ Trim the asparagus, peel if necessary and cut into 1-inch pieces.

▼ Bring 1 inch salted water to a boil in a medium skillet. Add the asparagus. Cook for 3 minutes or until tender; drain and set aside.

▼ Heat the olive oil in a large skillet over medium heat. Add the shrimp. Cook for 3 minutes or until the shrimp turn pink; do not overcook. Remove the shrimp from the skillet. Set the skillet aside.

▼ Cook the penne al dente according to the package directions; drain, rinse and drain.

▼ Combine the shallots and the wine mixture in the large skillet. Bring to a boil. Heat until the liquid is evaporated.

▼ Add the whipping cream and broth. Simmer until reduced by half.

▼ Add the asparagus and shrimp, stirring to mix well.

▼ Simmer for 2 minutes. Add salt and pepper.

▼ Add the penne and toss until well mixed.

▼ Sprinkle with the chives and serve immediately.

Yield: 4 servings

Shrimp Alfredo

- ▼ Sauté the onion and garlic in the olive oil in a large skillet until tender.
- ▼ Blend a small amount of the milk with the flour in a small bowl. Stir into the mixture in the skillet. Cook until thickened, stirring constantly.
- ▼ Add the remaining milk, soup, salt, pepper, Parmesan cheese, broccoli and shrimp to the skillet.
- ▼ Cook until the sauce thickens and the shrimp turn pink, stirring constantly.
- ▼ Serve over the pasta.

Yield: 2 to 4 servings

1 small onion, chopped
1 clove of garlic, minced
1 teaspoon olive oil
2 cups skim milk
3 tablespoons flour
1 (10-ounce) can cream of
    chicken soup
1/2 teaspoon salt
1/4 teaspoon pepper
1/2 cup grated Parmesan cheese
16 ounces broccoli florets
1 cup peeled deveined shrimp
8 ounces favorite pasta, cooked

Shrimp Tempura

- ▼ Combine the biscuit mix and cornstarch in a bowl. Add enough water to make a thin batter.
- ▼ Dip the shrimp into the batter.
- ▼ Deep-fry in oil preheated to 375 degrees until golden brown; shrimp will rise to the surface.

Yield: 6 to 8 servings

1/2 cup biscuit mix
1/2 cup cornstarch
1/2 cup (or more) water
2 to 3 pounds peeled fresh shrimp
Peanut oil or vegetable oil for
    deep-frying

Shrimp Tetrazzini

▼ Cook the macaroni according to the package directions. Drain, rinse with cold water, drain well and set aside.

▼ Cook the shrimp in boiling salted water just until the shrimp turn pink. Drain and cool.

▼ Peel and devein the shrimp. Cut into pieces as desired and set aside.

▼ Sauté the green pepper and onion in the butter in a skillet until tender.

▼ Combine the soups and evaporated milk in a large bowl and mix well. Add the macaroni, shrimp, sautéed vegetables and ¼ cup of the cheese and mix well.

▼ Pour into a lightly greased large casserole.

▼ Top with the remaining cheese and a layer of cracker crumbs.

▼ Drizzle the melted margarine over the crumbs.

▼ Bake at 350 degrees for 20 to 30 minutes or until bubbly and golden brown.

Yield: 6 to 8 servings

12 ounces shell or elbow macaroni
2 pounds shrimp
Salt to taste
⅓ cup chopped green bell pepper
½ cup chopped onion
¼ cup butter
1 (10-ounce) can cream of celery soup
1 (10-ounce) can cream of mushroom soup
1 cup evaporated milk
1¼ cups (or more) shredded mild Cheddar cheese
1 cup (or more) crushed butter crackers
2 tablespoons melted margarine

Free Lunch at the Palace Saloon

*I*n the early 1900s Mr. Lewis Hirth, owner of the Palace Saloon, served free lunch to his customers at a buffet set up on the far north end of the bar. The shrimp were provided by Mr. "A" Mitchell who had a seafood business close by, where he boiled the shrimp in a large pot outside.

Often Mr. Hirth would stroll over to taste the shrimp. The text of their conversation never changed. Mr. Mitchell would ask "how do you like the shrimp Louie?" and Mr. Hirth's reply would be "Not enough salt "A," you gotta put in more salt." Of course the idea being the saltier the shrimp the thirstier his lunch guests would be.

Shrimp and Artichoke Casserole

▼ Cook the pasta according to the package directions. Drain, rinse with cold water, drain well and set aside.

▼ Cook the shrimp, peel, devein and set aside.

▼ Melt 4½ tablespoons butter in a saucepan. Add the flour and blend well.

▼ Stir in the milk and half-and-half gradually. Cook until thickened, stirring constantly. Remove from the heat. Add salt and pepper.

▼ Sauté the mushrooms in 2 tablespoons butter in a skillet. Add the sherry and Worcestershire sauce, mix well and set aside.

▼ Place the pasta in a greased casserole. Drain and chop the artichokes and layer over the pasta.

▼ Arrange the shrimp on the artichokes. Pour the sauce over the top, sprinkle with Parmesan cheese and paprika.

▼ Bake at 375 degrees for 20 minutes.

Yield: 6 servings

6 ounces pasta
1 pound shrimp
4½ tablespoons butter
4½ tablespoons flour
¾ cup milk
¾ cup half-and-half
Salt and pepper to taste
4 ounces fresh mushrooms, sliced
2 tablespoons butter
¼ cup sherry
1 tablespoon Worcestershire sauce
1 (13-ounce) can artichoke hearts
½ cup grated Parmesan cheese
Paprika to taste

Abundance of Shrimp

No wonder the modern shrimping industry became successful. Earliest U.S. Government fishery statistics (1879–1880) stated of Fernandina: ". . . shrimp and prawns are abundant in the harbor directly opposite the city during the entire year, and a man can readily secure 3 or 4 bushels with a small cast net on any pleasant night."

Centre Attractions

Entrées

Waterfront

The peaceful vista of the Amelia River, sprinkled with a few sailboats, shrimp-boats, and an occasional frolicking porpoise or loggerhead turtle, is a far cry from the hustle and bustle of the waterfront scene of Fernandina's Golden Era (1873–1910). Before modern dredging techniques were developed at the turn of this century, Fernandina possessed the best deep-water harbor on the South Atlantic Coast of the United States.

Not only was the harbor only 2.5 miles from the open water, but even at low tide the largest of the wooden vessels could come and go at will because there were at least seventeen feet of water beneath their keels. Early accounts claim that the harbor was large enough for four hundred ships to swing on anchor. When the United States passed the Embargo Act of 1807 closing its ports to foreign trade, Amelia Island, then a Spanish possession, became the busiest port in the Western Hemisphere. Fernandina and Tampa were the only two ports of entry in Florida after statehood was granted in 1845.

With the advent of the first trans-Florida railroad shortly after the War Between the States, Fernandina became a busy rail-sea trans-shipment point as Florida logs, turpentine, and other raw materials were loaded on steamships bound for New York and Europe. Manufactured goods arrived in Florida via the port of Fernandina. As the first east coast Florida tourist resort, Fernandina was the first glimpse many visitors from the North got of Florida as passenger steamers docked there. Lumber-yards, barrel makers, and icehouses dotted the waterfront during the heyday of Fernandina's Golden Age.

Montana Mulligan Stew

This recipe will serve three Murphys, two O'Sullivans and a token Norwegian.

▼ Peel the carrots. Cut the carrots and beef into 1-inch chunks.

▼ Combine the carrots, beef, celery, tomatoes and bread cubes in a bowl.

▼ Sprinkle the soup mix, tapioca, sherry, sugar, salt, pepper and herbs over the vegetables and beef and mix well. Spoon into a greased 9x13-inch baking pan.

▼ Bake, tightly covered with foil, at 250 degrees for about 4¾ hours.

▼ Stir the peas into the stew.

▼ Bake, uncovered, for about 20 minutes longer.

Yield: 6 to 8 servings

6 large carrots
2 pounds beef stew meat
1 cup chopped celery
1 (16-ounce) can tomatoes
2 slices white bread, cubed
1 envelope onion soup mix
3 tablespoons quick-cooking
   tapioca
½ cup sherry or wine
1 tablespoon sugar
1 teaspoon salt
¼ teaspoon pepper
¼ teaspoon each thyme,
   rosemary and marjoram
1 (10-ounce) package frozen
   green peas

Spanish Beef

1½ pounds beef stew meat
2 slices bacon, chopped
1 large onion, chopped
1 small clove of garlic, finely
   chopped
1 (20-ounce) can tomatoes
1 (8-ounce) can tomato sauce
1 tablespoon chili powder
1 teaspoon salt
1 teaspoon pepper
½ cup red wine
1 cup sliced pimento-stuffed
   green olives
8 servings hot cooked rice

▼ Cut the beef into small cubes. (If the beef was purchased already cubed, each piece usually needs to be quartered.)
▼ Cook the beef with the bacon in a large heavy Dutch oven until well browned, stirring frequently.
▼ Add the onion, garlic, tomatoes, tomato sauce, chili powder, salt and pepper and mix well.
▼ Simmer, covered, for 1 to 1½ hours or until the beef is very tender, stirring occasionally.
▼ Add the wine and olives and mix well.
▼ Cook, covered, for 15 to 20 minutes longer.
▼ Serve over rice with a tossed green salad and hot rolls.

Yield: 8 servings

Port of Fernandina and the Cuban Revolution of 1896

The official position of the United States was neutral at the beginning of the Cuban Revolution with the navy patrolling the Atlantic seaboard to prevent smuggling. However, that did not stop the adventurous spirited seamen and merchants in Fernandina.

The many Cubans in Florida had roused public sentiment and a lively filibustering trade was built up with Cuba, whose troubles with Spain had long been fomenting. Arms, ammunition, and recruits for the rebel Cuban army were regularly shipped out of Fernandina.

In spite of the danger, a number of vessels, including the *Dauntless*, *La Gonda*, *Three Friends*, *Commodore*, and *Paul Jones* operated from the Port of Fernandina. These creative businessmen were gallantly "rallying to the cause" as well as adding to their own fortunes.

Beef Stroganoff with a Kick

Don't be alarmed by the addition of the jalapeños. The sour cream will tone down the heat but leave a terrific taste (unless you add too many jalapeños).

▼ Cut the beef into ½x1½-inch strips.

▼ Cook the beef strips in the margarine in a large skillet over low heat until brown, stirring occasionally.

▼ Reserve ⅓ cup of the broth. Stir the remaining broth, ketchup, salt and garlic into the skillet.

▼ Bring the mixture to a boil and reduce heat to a simmer. Simmer, covered, for 10 minutes or until the beef is tender.

▼ Add the mushrooms, onion and jalapeños. Simmer, covered, for 5 minutes or until the onion is tender.

▼ Blend the reserved broth with the flour. Stir into the beef mixture gradually. Cook for 1 minute or until thickened, stirring constantly.

▼ Stir in the sour cream. Heat to serving temperature but do not boil.

▼ Serve over the noodles or rice.

Yield: 6 servings

1½ pounds beef tenderloin or top loin, sliced ½ inch thick
2 tablespoons margarine
1½ cups beef broth
2 tablespoons ketchup
1 teaspoon salt
1 small clove of garlic, finely chopped
8 ounces fresh mushrooms, sliced
½ cup chopped onion
½ to 1 cup chopped jalapeños
3 tablespoons flour
1 cup sour cream
6 servings hot cooked noodles or rice

Slow-Cooker Stroganoff

3 pounds round steak
½ cup flour
2 teaspoons salt
⅛ teaspoon pepper
2 large onions
2 (4-ounce) cans mushrooms
1 (10-ounce) can beef consommé
1½ cups sour cream
¼ cup flour
8 servings hot cooked noodles

▼ Trim the steak and cut into thin strips. Coat the strips evenly with ½ cup flour and place in a slow cooker. Season with the salt and pepper.

▼ Slice the onions thinly and separate into rings. Place onions, drained mushrooms and consommé in the cooker.

▼ Cook, covered, on Low for 8 to 10 hours.

▼ Turn the cooker off and let stand for about 30 minutes.

▼ Stir a mixture of the sour cream and ¼ cup flour into the cooker. Serve the stroganoff over the noodles.

Yield: 8 servings

Fernandina's First Auto Accident

The first accident of anything like a serious nature caused by an automobile to occur in Fernandina was that of last Friday afternoon, when Mr. Fred McCarl was struck by a car belonging to Mayor N. B. Borden, the occupants of the car being Mrs. N. B. Borden and her two lady guests, the Misses Ryan, of Brooklyn, N.Y. . . .

It seems that Mr. McCarl had started across Fourth Street to the postoffice only a few steps from Centre, when the automobile, either through lack of control or fright of the impending accident on the part of the driver [one of the Misses Ryan], made a wide turn to the left side of fourth street and right toward Mr. McCarl who, no doubt, becoming excited at the approaching danger, failed in his efforts to dodge the car, and was struck with serious results, which at the time, were feared would prove fatal, but at this time such fears have been dispelled. . . .

The accident was a very regrettable occurrence by all, but of course by none more than the occupants of the car, whose grief and nervousness almost overcame them at the time and they are administering to the relief of the victim of the accident in every possible manner.

Mr. McCarl is one of the assistants in the post office here and his efficient service will be greatly missed during the time of his recovery. He is also organist at the Methodist church of this city and here, too, his enforced absence due to his injuries will be sadly felt. . . .

from *Fernandina News-Record*, February 16, 1912

Farmhouse Barbecue-Filled Muffins

▼ Separate the dough into 10 biscuits. Flatten each biscuit into a 5-inch circle.

▼ Press each circle over the bottom and up the side of a greased muffin cup.

▼ Cook the ground beef in a skillet until brown and crumbly, stirring frequently; drain well.

▼ Combine the ketchup, brown sugar, vinegar and chili powder in a small bowl and mix well. Stir into the ground beef.

▼ Spoon about 1/4 cup of the ground beef mixture into each biscuit-lined muffin cup. Sprinkle with the cheese.

▼ Bake at 375 degrees for 18 to 20 minutes or until golden brown.

▼ Cool in the pan for 5 minutes before removing and serving.

Yield: 10 servings

1 (10-count) can refrigerated buttermilk biscuits
1 pound ground beef
1/2 cup ketchup
3 tablespoons brown sugar
1 tablespoon cider vinegar
1/2 teaspoon chili powder
1 cup shredded Cheddar cheese

Barry's Firehouse Chili

1 pound (or more) ground beef
2 (16-ounce) cans (or more) kidney beans
1 (6-ounce) can (or more) tomato paste
½ (or more) onion, chopped
1 (or more) green bell pepper, chopped
Small dash of ground red pepper

FIRST ALARM

▼ Cook the ground beef in a large stockpot until brown and crumbly, stirring frequently; drain.

▼ Add the undrained kidney beans, tomato paste, onion, green pepper and seasoning and mix well.

▼ Simmer, covered, until ready to eat.

SECOND ALARM

▼ Same ingredients as above except use a medium dash of red pepper.

▼ After combining all the ingredients as above, cook as long as you dare.

▼ Call 911 and ask for the Fire Department. Suggest they bring a fire hose to put out the fire in your stomach.

▼ Be sure you have extra towels for mopping your brow while eating and afterwards.

THIRD ALARM

▼ Same ingredients and method as above except use a medium dash of red pepper and a small dash of cayenne.

GENERAL ALARM

▼ Same ingredients and method as above except use a large dash of red pepper, a large dash of cayenne and 1 tablespoon jalapeño sauce or juice.

Yield: 4 (or more) servings

Stuffed Pasta Shells

- ▼ Cook the pasta shells according to the package directions; drain and set aside.
- ▼ Brown the ground beef with the onion in a large skillet, stirring until the ground beef is crumbly; drain.
- ▼ Add the black pepper, garlic powder and red pepper and mix well. Cover and set aside.
- ▼ Combine the broth, tomatoes, pine nuts, basil, 2 tablespoons parsley and garlic in a blender container. Process until smooth.
- ▼ Add the olive oil in a fine stream, processing constantly.
- ▼ Pour the broth mixture into the ground beef mixture and mix well. Stir in the Parmesan cheese.
- ▼ Stuff each pasta shell with a heaping tablespoon of the ground beef mixture.
- ▼ Arrange the stuffed shells in a lightly greased 9x13-inch baking dish.
- ▼ Pour the spaghetti sauce over the shells.
- ▼ Bake, covered, at 375 degrees for 20 to 30 minutes.
- ▼ Sprinkle with the mozzarella cheese.
- ▼ Bake, uncovered, for 5 minutes longer or until the cheese melts.
- ▼ Sprinkle 1 to 2 tablespoons chopped parsley over the top.

Yield: 12 servings

24 jumbo pasta shells
1 pound ground beef
1/2 cup minced onion
1/2 teaspoon black pepper
1/4 teaspoon garlic powder
1/4 teaspoon crushed red pepper
1 1/4 cups beef broth
1 (7-ounce) jar oil-pack sun-dried tomatoes, drained
1/4 cup pine nuts, toasted
1/4 cup fresh basil
2 tablespoons chopped fresh parsley
2 cloves of garlic, sliced
1/4 cup olive oil
1/3 cup grated Parmesan cheese
1 (32-ounce) jar spaghetti sauce
1 1/2 cups shredded mozzarella cheese
1 to 2 tablespoons chopped fresh parsley

Oven Jambalaya

1 pound bacon
2½ pounds uncooked peeled
  shrimp
1 pound smoked sausage
1 (10-ounce) can beef bouillon
1 (10-ounce) can French onion
  soup
1 (8-ounce) can tomato sauce
½ cup melted butter
1½ cups chopped green bell
  pepper
½ cup chopped fresh parsley
½ cup chopped onion
½ cup chopped celery
8 ounces fresh mushrooms,
  chopped
2 cloves of garlic, crushed
2 cups uncooked rice
1 (7-ounce) can sliced water
  chestnuts
1 tablespoon Konriko Creole
  seasoning

This recipe is excellent for a crowd. Add salad and bread for a complete meal.

▼ Cook the bacon in a skillet until crisp; drain and crumble.
▼ Combine the bacon and shrimp in a large deep baking pan.
▼ Cut the sausage into bite-size pieces and add to the pan.
▼ Add the bouillon, soup, tomato sauce and melted butter and mix well.
▼ Stir in the green pepper, parsley, onion, celery and mushrooms. Add the garlic, rice, water chestnuts and Creole seasoning and mix well.
▼ Bake, covered, at 350 degrees for 1½ hours, stirring occasionally.

Yield: 15 servings

Supreme of Chicken Aloha

Located in the Palmetto Walk Shopping Village, The Alpine Market serves the south end of the island wonderful creative cuisine. Try this special recipe.

▼ Rinse the chicken and pat dry. Pound the chicken breast between waxed paper to flatten.

▼ Coat the chicken with 2 tablespoons flour and dip into the beaten egg.

▼ Roll the chicken in the coconut to coat completely and mold into an oval shape.

▼ Place the chicken in a sauté pan. Cook over low heat until golden brown on both sides.

▼ Remove to a small shallow baking dish. Bake at 275 degrees for 15 minutes or until cooked through.

▼ Melt the butter in a skillet. Add 1¼ cups flour and curry powder and blend well. Cook over low heat for several minutes, stirring frequently.

▼ Stir in the chicken broth and the desired amount of wine gradually. Cook until thickened, stirring constantly.

▼ Bring to a boil. Whisk in enough heavy cream to make the sauce of the desired consistency.

▼ Grill the pineapple slice.

▼ Nap the serving plate with about 6 tablespoons of the sauce. Place the chicken on the sauce.

▼ Top the chicken with the pineapple slice and chutney.

▼ Surround the chicken with fried or boiled plantains and serve immediately.

▼ May substitute other choices of meat or shrimp for the chicken.

Yield: 1 serving

1 (8-ounce) boneless skinless chicken breast
2 tablespoons (about) flour
1 egg, beaten
4 ounces shredded coconut
¾ cup butter
1¼ cups (scant) flour
Curry powder to taste
4 cups chicken broth
White wine to taste
Heavy cream to taste
1 pineapple slice or peach half
1 tablespoon mango chutney
Fried or boiled plantains or rice pilaf

Chicken Casserole

4 to 6 chicken breasts
1 (10-ounce) can cream of
    chicken soup
1 (10-ounce) can cream of
    mushroom soup
1 cup sour cream
1 (14-ounce) can artichoke
    hearts, drained, chopped
2 (8-ounce) cans sliced
    mushrooms, drained
2 stacks Ritz crackers, finely
    crushed
1/2 cup melted butter

▼ Remove and discard chicken skin and rinse the chicken. Cook in water to cover in a saucepan until tender.
▼ Drain the chicken, discard bones and cut into desired size cubes.
▼ Combine the chicken, soups, sour cream, artichokes and mushrooms in a bowl and mix gently. Combine the cracker crumbs and melted butter in a medium bowl and mix well.
▼ Spread about 2/3 of the crumb mixture in a lightly greased 9x11-inch baking dish.
▼ Spoon the chicken mixture over the crumb mixture. Top with the remaining crumb mixture.
▼ Bake, covered, at 350 degrees for 40 minutes. Bake, uncovered, for 5 to 10 minutes longer or until bubbly.

Yield: 6 to 8 servings

Grilled Chicken Teriyaki

2 to 3 pounds boneless skinless
    chicken breasts
1/2 cup soy sauce
1/2 cup vegetable oil
1/4 cup pineapple juice
2 cloves of garlic, minced
1 tablespoon (or more) brown
    sugar
1 teaspoon ground ginger
1 tablespoon grated orange or
    lemon peel
4 to 6 servings hot cooked rice

▼ Rinse the chicken and pat dry. Cut the chicken into strips and place in a bowl.
▼ Mix the soy sauce, oil, pineapple juice, garlic, brown sugar, ginger and orange peel in a small bowl. Pour the marinade over the chicken and mix until coated.
▼ Marinate, covered, in the refrigerator for 3 to 5 hours, stirring occasionally. Drain the chicken. Thread the chicken onto skewers.
▼ Grill over hot coals until the juices run clear when the chicken is pierced with a fork, turning occasionally.
▼ Serve over the rice.

Yield: 4 to 6 servings

Chicken Curry

▼ Rinse the chicken and pat dry. Place in a baking dish.

▼ Bake at 350 degrees for 1½ hours.

▼ Discard the skin and bones and cut the chicken into bite-size pieces. Set aside.

▼ Sauté the green peppers in the butter in a large skillet until tender.

▼ Add the onions. Sauté until tender.

▼ Add the flour, salt and curry powder. Cook for several minutes, stirring constantly.

▼ Stir in the chicken stock and tomatoes. Cook until thickened, stirring constantly. Add the Worcestershire sauce, steak sauce, Kitchen Bouquet and honey.

▼ Stir in the chicken pieces. Pour into a large baking dish.

▼ Bake at 350 degrees for about 45 minutes.

▼ Serve over the rice.

Yield: 8 servings

4 **whole chicken breasts**
3 **green bell peppers, chopped**
5 **to 6 tablespoons butter**
3 **onions, chopped**
6 **tablespoons flour**
1½ **teaspoons salt**
1 **tablespoon curry powder**
1½ **cups chicken stock**
4 **(15-ounce) cans tomatoes**
1½ **tablespoons Worcestershire sauce**
1 **tablespoon A.1. steak sauce**
1 **tablespoon Kitchen Bouquet**
1 **tablespoon honey**
8 **servings hot cooked rice**

Drunken Chicken

**8 boneless skinless chicken
  breasts**
Salt and pepper to taste
¼ cup margarine
**2 (10-ounce) cans cream of
  chicken soup**
1½ cups sauterne
1 (7-ounce) can water chestnuts
**2 (3-ounce) cans sliced
  mushrooms, drained**
**¼ cup chopped green bell
  peppers**
¼ teaspoon thyme

▼ Rinse the chicken and pat dry. Sprinkle with salt and
  pepper.
▼ Cook the chicken in the margarine in a skillet over low
  heat until light brown. Remove chicken to a baking dish.
▼ Add the soup and wine to the skillet. Bring to a boil,
  stirring until well mixed.
▼ Drain the water chestnuts and slice thinly. Add to the
  skillet.
▼ Add the mushrooms, green peppers and thyme and
  mix well.
▼ Spoon the sauce over the chicken. Cover tightly with foil.
▼ Bake at 350 degrees for 45 minutes.
▼ Bake, uncovered, for 30 minutes longer.
▼ May prepare a day ahead and refrigerate. Bake, covered,
  for 1 hour; bake, uncovered, for 15 minutes.

Yield: 8 servings

Chicken Stir-Fry

▼ Rinse the chicken and pat dry. Cut into bite-size pieces.

▼ Combine the soy sauce, garlic and cornstarch in a 1-cup measure and mix until the cornstarch dissolves. Add enough water to measure 1 cup.

▼ Slice the carrots.

▼ Cut the broccoli and cauliflower into bite-size pieces.

▼ Slice the onion; chop coarsely.

▼ Heat the olive oil in a wok or heavy skillet over medium-high heat.

▼ Add the chicken. Stir-fry until the chicken is opaque and almost cooked through.

▼ Add the carrots. Stir-fry until almost tender.

▼ Add the broccoli, cauliflower and onion. Stir-fry for 2 minutes.

▼ Stir the soy sauce mixture into the wok. Cook until the sauce is clear and slightly thickened, stirring constantly. Do not overcook.

▼ Serve over the rice. Sprinkle with chow mein noodles.

Yield: 6 servings

5 boneless skinless chicken breasts
¼ cup soy sauce
2 cloves of garlic, minced
2 tablespoons cornstarch
3 carrots
1 bunch broccoli
½ head cauliflower
1 large onion
2 tablespoons extra-light olive oil
6 servings hot cooked rice
1 cup (or more) chow mein noodles

Italian Chicken Casserole

8 ounces fettuccini
4 boneless skinless chicken breasts
1 cup sliced mushrooms
¼ cup minced onion
1 tablespoon butter
1 cup white wine
1 cup whipping cream
1 tablespoon butter
¼ teaspoon salt
¼ teaspoon pepper
¼ teaspoon garlic powder
¼ cup grated Parmesan cheese
2 cups shredded mozzarella cheese

▼ Cook the fettuccini al dente according to the package directions; drain. Rinse with cold water and drain well.

▼ Rinse the chicken and pat dry. Cut the chicken into strips.

▼ Sauté the chicken, mushrooms and onion in 1 tablespoon butter in a large skillet until the chicken is tender and slightly browned.

▼ Add the wine and mix well. Simmer, covered, until almost dry.

▼ Scald the cream in a small saucepan. Add 1 tablespoon butter, salt, pepper and garlic powder and stir until the butter melts.

▼ Place the fettuccini in a 2-quart baking dish. Sprinkle with the Parmesan cheese.

▼ Pour the cream mixture over the fettuccini and add the chicken mixture.

▼ Sprinkle with the mozzarella cheese.

▼ Bake at 350 degrees for 20 minutes or until the cheese is bubbly and light brown.

Yield: 4 servings

Chicken Lasagna

▼ Cook the noodles according to the package directions; drain. Rinse and drain well.

▼ Melt the margarine in a large saucepan over medium heat. Add the flour and blend well. Add the salt, pepper and basil and mix well. Cook for 1 to 2 minutes, stirring constantly.

▼ Stir in the broth. Bring to a boil, stirring constantly. Reduce the heat.

▼ Cook for 5 to 8 minutes longer or until thickened, stirring constantly.

▼ Stir in the chicken and remove from the heat.

▼ Combine the cottage cheese and egg in a bowl and mix well.

▼ Layer 1/3 of the chicken mixture, half the noodles, half the cottage cheese mixture and half the mozzarella cheese in a lightly greased 9x13-inch baking dish.

▼ Repeat the layers. Top with the remaining chicken mixture.

▼ Sprinkle with the Parmesan cheese.

▼ Bake at 350 degrees for 1 hour.

Yield: 8 servings

8 ounces medium noodles
1/2 cup margarine
1/2 cup flour
1 teaspoon salt
1/2 teaspoon pepper
1 teaspoon basil
4 cups chicken broth
4 cups chopped cooked chicken
24 ounces cottage cheese
1 egg
2 cups shredded mozzarella cheese
3/4 cup grated Parmesan cheese

Chicken Pesto Pasta

1 large chicken
16 ounces ziti
Pesto Sauce
Salt to taste
Pine nuts to taste

▼ Rinse the chicken and pat dry. Roast the chicken until tender.

▼ Let the chicken cool enough to handle. Remove and discard the skin and bones.

▼ Cut the chicken into bite-size pieces.

▼ Cook the ziti according to the package directions and drain well.

▼ Combine the hot ziti, chicken, Pesto Sauce, salt and pine nuts in a large bowl and toss to mix.

▼ Serve immediately.

Pesto Sauce

2 cups chopped fresh basil leaves
1/2 cup olive oil
2 teaspoons chopped garlic
1/2 cup grated Parmesan cheese
3 tablespoons pine nuts

▼ Combine the basil, olive oil, garlic, Parmesan cheese and pine nuts in a blender or food processor container.

▼ Process until smooth and of sauce consistency.

Yield: 8 servings

Greek Pizza

▼ Rinse the spinach well; discard the stems and chop.

▼ Sauté the onion and garlic in 2 tablespoons olive oil in a large skillet until the onion is tender.

▼ Add the basil, oregano, salt, pepper, lemon juice and spinach. Cook over medium-high heat until the spinach is wilted and the mixture is almost dry.

▼ Butter a large baking sheet. Blend the melted butter with ¼ cup olive oil.

▼ Layer the phyllo on the prepared baking sheet, brushing each layer with the butter mixture. Brush the top with the remaining butter mixture.

▼ Remove the spinach mixture from the skillet with a slotted spoon. Spread the spinach mixture over the phyllo, leaving a ½-inch edge.

▼ Sprinkle the feta cheese and half the mozzarella cheese over the spinach.

▼ Slice the tomatoes thinly. Coat both sides of the tomato slices with bread crumbs. Arrange the tomato slices over the mozzarella cheese.

▼ Sprinkle with the remaining mozzarella cheese.

▼ Bake at 400 degrees for 25 to 30 minutes or until the pizza is golden brown.

▼ May substitute one 10-ounce package frozen chopped spinach for the fresh spinach.

Yield: 4 to 6 servings

1 pound fresh spinach
1 cup chopped onion
3 large cloves of garlic, crushed
2 tablespoons olive oil
½ teaspoon basil
½ teaspoon oregano
¼ teaspoon salt
Freshly ground pepper to taste
Juice of ½ large lemon
½ cup melted butter
¼ cup olive oil
8 ounces phyllo dough
1½ cups crumbled feta cheese
4 cups shredded mozzarella cheese
2 medium tomatoes
1 cup (about) bread crumbs

Mexican Pizza

▼ Drain the beans. Combine with the olive oil, parsley, cumin and garlic in a food processor or blender container. Process until smooth, scraping the sides of the container as necessary.

▼ Bake the pizza crust at 425 degrees for about 10 minutes or until firm but not brown.

▼ Spread the bean mixture over the partially baked pizza crust.

▼ Sprinkle with the cheeses.

▼ Drain the olives well. Sprinkle the olives, green pepper and green onions over the cheeses.

▼ Bake for 8 to 12 minutes longer or until the crust is golden brown and the cheeses are melted.

▼ Serve with salsa and sour cream.

Yield: 4 to 6 servings

1 (16-ounce) can black beans
3 tablespoons olive oil or
    canola oil
2 tablespoons minced fresh
    parsley
1 teaspoon ground cumin
1/2 teaspoon minced garlic
1 (12-inch) pizza crust
2 cups mixed shredded Cheddar
    and Monterey Jack cheeses
1 (2-ounce) can sliced black
    olives
1/2 cup chopped green bell pepper
1/4 cup sliced green onions
Salsa to taste
Sour cream to taste

Spinach Lasagna

This recipe is delicious made with light spaghetti sauce and low-fat cheeses.

▼ Rinse the spinach well; discard the stems and chop. Cook the spinach in a small amount of boiling water until tender; drain well.

▼ Cook the lasagna noodles according to the package directions; drain. Rinse and drain well.

▼ Sauté the garlic, mushrooms and onion in the olive oil in a large skillet until tender.

▼ Add the salt and spinach and mix well.

▼ Combine the ricotta cheese with the egg in a bowl and mix well.

▼ Layer the noodles, spinach mixture, ricotta mixture, mozzarella cheese and spaghetti sauce ½ at a time in a lightly greased 9x13-inch baking dish.

▼ Sprinkle with Parmesan cheese.

▼ Bake at 400 degrees for 45 minutes.

▼ May substitute one 16-ounce package frozen chopped spinach for the fresh spinach.

Yield: 6 to 8 servings

1 large package fresh spinach
6 to 8 lasagna noodles
2 cloves of garlic, minced
1 pound fresh mushrooms, sliced
1 small onion, chopped
3 tablespoons olive oil
½ teaspoon salt
1 cup ricotta cheese
1 egg
2 cups shredded mozzarella cheese
1 (28-ounce) jar spaghetti sauce
Parmesan cheese to taste

Fortifications

Side Dishes

Fort Clinch

Fort Clinch was named for General Duncan Lamont Clinch, a leader of the Second Seminole War. Construction on the fort is thought to have begun in 1847 but was never completed. When the War Between the States began in 1861, only two of the five bastions had been completed, along with two walls, the ramparts, the guardhouse, and the prison.

At the beginning of the war (April 1861) the Confederates seized the fort. In 1862, General Robert E. Lee ordered it evacuated when he determined that it could not be properly defended. When the Union troops regained the fort, efforts were made to complete construction. The construction work on Fort Clinch was completely stopped in 1867. The invention of the rifled cannon and more powerful gunpowder made the fort's brick construction obsolete. The new weaponry would have shattered the brick into deadly shrapnel.

The fort was briefly reactivated in 1898 during the Spanish-American War and again during World War II for surveillance and communications.

Fort Clinch is now a Florida State Park, with 1,086 acres for camping, tours, and exploring.

Easy Asparagus Vinaigrette

▼ Combine the olive oil, vinegar, basil, salt, sugar and pepper in a small jar. Shake vigorously and set aside.

▼ Rinse the asparagus and snap off the tough ends.

▼ Place the asparagus in a steamer basket over boiling water. Steam, covered, for 4 to 6 minutes or just until tender-crisp.

▼ Arrange the asparagus on a serving platter. Sprinkle with the chopped tomato.

▼ Drizzle the vinaigrette over the asparagus.

▼ Garnish with the basil sprigs and serve immediately.

Yield: 4 servings

2 tablespoons olive oil
2 tablespoons cider vinegar
2 tablespoons chopped fresh basil
1/2 teaspoon salt
1/4 teaspoon sugar
1/8 teaspoon pepper
1 pound fresh asparagus spears
1/3 cup chopped tomato
Fresh basil sprigs

Company Baked Beans

▼ Brown the ground beef with the onion and green pepper in a large skillet over medium-high heat, stirring until the ground beef is crumbly; drain well.

▼ Add the beans, picante sauce, brown sugar, mustard and Worcestershire sauce and mix well.

▼ Bring to a boil, stirring frequently.

▼ Pour into a 9x13-inch baking dish sprayed with nonstick cooking spray.

▼ Bake at 350 degrees for 1 hour or until bubbly.

Yield: 10 to 12 servings

1 pound ground beef
1 large onion, chopped
1 large green bell pepper, chopped
3 (16-ounce) cans baked beans
1 1/2 cups picante sauce
1/4 cup packed brown sugar
1 tablespoon prepared mustard
1 tablespoon Worcestershire sauce

Black Bean Enchiladas

1 clove of garlic, minced
1 tablespoon vegetable oil
1 (15-ounce) can black beans, drained
1 (16-ounce) can tomatoes, coarsely chopped
1 cup cooked rice
1/2 cup Enchilada Sauce
1 vegetable bouillon cube
1/3 cup water
1/2 teaspoon minced fresh oregano leaves
3/4 cup chopped green bell pepper
2 cups shredded Cheddar cheese
12 flour tortillas

If the vegetarian enchiladas are served as a main dish, garnish with avocado slices, sour cream and chopped green onions.

▼ Sauté the garlic in oil in a large skillet until tender but not brown.
▼ Add the beans, undrained tomatoes, rice, Enchilada Sauce, bouillon cube, water and oregano. Boil for 1 minute or until the bouillon cube dissolves, stirring constantly. Remove from the heat.
▼ Stir in the green pepper and 1 cup of the cheese.
▼ Spoon about 1/3 cup of the mixture onto each tortilla and roll up to enclose the filling. Place seam side down in a greased 9x13-inch baking dish. Spoon the remaining Enchilada Sauce on top.
▼ Bake, covered with foil, at 350 degrees for 20 minutes. Sprinkle with the remaining cheese.

Enchilada Sauce

1 (16-ounce) can tomatoes, chopped
1/2 cup chopped onion
2 tablespoons (or more) chopped jalapeños
1/2 teaspoon salt
1/2 cup chopped green bell pepper
1 teaspoon garlic powder
1 teaspoon minced fresh parsley or cilantro

▼ Simmer the undrained tomatoes in a medium saucepan until juices are thickened.
▼ Add the remaining ingredients and cook until the green pepper is tender-crisp, stirring frequently.

Yield: 6 servings

Creamy Cabbage Casserole

▼ Spread the cabbage evenly in a lightly greased 9x12-inch baking dish. Sprinkle with pepper.

▼ Peel, seed and chop the tomatoes. Sprinkle over the cabbage.

▼ Crumble the bacon over the tomatoes.

▼ Sauté the onion in 1 teaspoon butter in a skillet until tender. Spoon over the bacon and tomatoes.

▼ Melt the 2 tablespoons butter in a small saucepan. Blend in the flour and salt. Cook for 1 minute, stirring constantly.

▼ Stir in the milk gradually. Cook until thickened, stirring constantly, but do not allow the mixture to boil.

▼ Remove the sauce from the heat. Blend in the sour cream. Spoon over the onion layer.

▼ Sprinkle the cheese over the top.

▼ Bake, covered with foil, at 350 degrees for 30 minutes.

▼ Bake, uncovered, for 20 minutes longer.

Yield: 8 servings

6 cups shredded cabbage
$\frac{1}{8}$ teaspoon coarsely ground pepper
2 large tomatoes
4 slices crisp-cooked bacon
1 large onion, chopped
1 teaspoon butter or bacon drippings
2 tablespoons butter
2 tablespoons flour
$\frac{1}{4}$ teaspoon salt
$\frac{1}{2}$ cup milk
$\frac{1}{2}$ cup sour cream, at room temperature
$1\frac{1}{2}$ cups shredded Monterey Jack or mozzarella cheese

Scalloped Corn and Tomatoes

2 (15-ounce) cans tomatoes,
  drained, chopped
1 (15-ounce) can whole kernel
  corn, drained
1 (15-ounce) can cream-style
  corn
2 eggs, slightly beaten
¼ cup flour
2 teaspoons sugar
1 teaspoon pepper
1 medium onion, finely chopped
½ teaspoon garlic powder
⅓ cup margarine or butter
4 cups soft bread crumbs
½ cup grated Parmesan cheese

▼ Combine the tomatoes, whole kernel corn, cream-style corn and eggs in a bowl and mix well. Spoon into a lightly greased 2-quart casserole.

▼ Add the flour, sugar and pepper and mix well.

▼ Sauté the onion with the garlic powder in the margarine in a skillet until the onion is tender but not brown. Remove from the heat.

▼ Add the bread crumbs and Parmesan cheese and mix until the crumbs are coated.

▼ Sprinkle the crumb mixture over the corn mixture.

▼ Bake at 350 degrees for about 1 hour or until set and golden brown.

Yield: 12 servings

Vidalia Onion and Rice Deep-Dish Casserole

▼ Bring the water to a boil in a medium saucepan. Stir in the rice. Simmer, covered, for 10 minutes. Drain and set aside.

▼ Sauté the onions in the butter in a large skillet over medium heat for 15 minutes. Remove from the heat.

▼ Add the rice, parsley, salt and white pepper and mix well. Add the cheese and whipping cream and mix well.

▼ Spoon into a lightly greased 9x13-inch baking dish.

▼ Bake, covered, at 350 degrees for 30 minutes.

▼ Sprinkle lightly with paprika before serving.

Yield: 10 servings

2 cups water
1 cup uncooked long grain rice
6 large Vidalia onions, chopped
¹/₂ cup butter or margarine
2 tablespoons chopped fresh parsley
¹/₄ teaspoon salt
¹/₄ teaspoon white pepper
1 cup shredded Swiss cheese
1 cup whipping cream
Paprika to taste

Vidalia Onion Pie

▼ Melt ¹/₄ cup margarine in a 9x9-inch baking dish.

▼ Add the cracker crumbs and mix well. Pat lightly over the bottom of the baking dish.

▼ Sauté the onions in 2 tablespoons margarine in a large skillet until tender. Mix in the salt and pepper.

▼ Spoon the onions into the prepared baking dish.

▼ Beat the eggs in a small bowl. Add the milk and beat until well blended.

▼ Pour the egg mixture over the onions.

▼ Sprinkle the cheese over the top.

▼ Bake at 350 degrees for 35 minutes or until set and golden brown.

Yield: 6 servings

¹/₄ cup margarine
1 cup saltine cracker crumbs
3 cups sliced Vidalia onions
2 tablespoons margarine
Salt and pepper to taste
2 eggs
³/₄ cup milk
¹/₄ cup shredded Cheddar cheese

Onion Squares

1 large Vidalia onion
1/4 cup margarine or butter
1 cup sour cream
1 teaspoon dried dillweed
1/2 teaspoon salt
1/4 teaspoon pepper
1 cup shredded sharp Cheddar
   cheese
1 cup corn muffin mix
1 egg
1/3 cup milk
2 dashes of Tabasco sauce
1 cup canned cream-style corn

This recipe can be prepared in a low-fat version by using low-fat or nonfat sour cream, cheese and milk.

▼ Slice the onion thinly. Sauté the onion in the margarine in a large skillet until clear. Remove from the heat.
▼ Add the sour cream, dillweed, salt, pepper and 1/2 cup of the cheese and mix gently.
▼ Combine the corn muffin mix, egg, milk, Tabasco sauce and corn in a medium bowl and mix well.
▼ Pour the batter into a greased 8x8-inch baking pan.
▼ Spoon the onion mixture over the batter and press into the batter lightly with the back of a spoon.
▼ Sprinkle with the remaining 1/2 cup cheese.
▼ Bake at 425 degrees for 25 to 30 minutes or until golden brown.
▼ Let stand for 10 minutes before cutting into squares.

Yield: 6 to 8 servings

Blue or Gray?

*A*lthough it was of strategic importance, Fort Clinch did not play a major role in the War Between the States. Apparently, neither side ever engaged the fort's guns in battle. Still, a soldier who served here, whether in gray or blue uniform, was often troubled with the same problems as those on the battlefield—sickness, boredom, and loneliness.

Roasted Garlic Mashed Potatoes

▼ Place the whole unpeeled garlic bulbs on a large sheet of foil. Drizzle the olive oil over the bulbs and seal in the foil.

▼ Bake at 425 degrees for 30 minutes. Set aside.

▼ Peel the potatoes and cut into 1-inch pieces. Place in a large saucepan and add water to cover.

▼ Bring to a boil. Cook for 15 to 20 minutes or until the potatoes are tender.

▼ Drain the potatoes and place in a large bowl. Add the butter, milk, salt and pepper. Beat with a mixer at medium speed until fluffy. Do not overbeat.

▼ Cut the pointed ends from the garlic and squeeze the pulp into the potatoes. Mix well with a spoon.

Yield: 8 servings

4 bulbs of garlic
1 tablespoon olive oil
4 pounds baking potatoes
$1/2$ cup butter or margarine
1 cup milk
$1^1/2$ teaspoons salt
$1/2$ teaspoon pepper

Bricks Tell Time

The most notable evidence of the different construction periods for Fort Clinch is the appearance of the bricks. The lower bricks were locally made before the War Between the States. The bricks above the rifle ports were imported from up North and set between 1862 and 1867.

Wild Mushroom Dauphinoise Potatoes

8 baking potatoes
2 cups shiitake mushrooms
2 cups oyster mushrooms
2 pints heavy cream
3 cups milk
8 eggs
2 cloves of garlic, chopped
1½ teaspoons salt
1 teaspoon pepper
1 cup grated Romano cheese

Try this wonderful recipe from Horizons, "Fine Dining in a Casual Atmosphere!," located in the Historic District. The recipe is easy, yet fantastic with any dish—beef, poultry, wild game or even seafood.

▼ Peel the potatoes and slice thinly. Set aside and cover with a damp cloth.

▼ Trim the mushrooms, removing the stems. Cut the mushrooms into thin strips and set aside.

▼ Combine the cream, milk, eggs, garlic, salt and pepper in a bowl and whisk until blended.

▼ Spray an 8x11-inch baking dish with nonstick cooking spray.

▼ Layer the potatoes and mushrooms in the baking dish. Pour the egg mixture over the layers.

▼ Sprinkle the cheese over the top.

▼ Bake, covered with foil, at 350 degrees for 30 to 35 minutes or until set.

▼ Bake, uncovered, for 10 minutes longer or until golden brown.

▼ Let stand for several minutes to cool slightly before serving.

Yield: 6 servings

Spinach Symphony

▼ Cook the spinach according to the package directions; drain well.
▼ Drain the artichoke hearts and mushrooms.
▼ Combine the soup, sour cream, mayonnaise and lemon juice in a large bowl and mix well. Add seasonings as desired.
▼ Fold in the spinach, artichokes and mushrooms.
▼ Pour into a lightly greased baking pan.
▼ Bake at 350 degrees for 25 to 30 minutes or until bubbly.

Yield: 10 servings

4 (10-ounce) packages frozen chopped spinach
2 (14-ounce) cans artichoke hearts
2 (4-ounce) cans mushrooms
2 (10-ounce) cans cream of mushroom soup
1 cup sour cream
3/4 cup mayonnaise
1 tablespoon lemon juice
Worcestershire sauce and Tabasco sauce to taste
Onion and garlic powder to taste
Salt to taste

But Whose Flag Flies Today?

General Clinch was first married on December 8, 1819, to Eliza Bayard McIntosh while stationed here in Fernandina. She was the daughter of John H. McIntosh, a prominent Georgian who was one of the so-called "Patriots of Amelia Island" who, with secret U.S. blessing, overthrew the Spanish and hoisted their own flag on March 17, 1812.

Acorn Squash Toss

1 acorn squash
Salt to taste
1 tablespoon olive oil
1 tablespoon butter or margarine
1 clove of garlic, minced
2 tablespoons soy sauce
2 teaspoons sesame seeds

The skin of the squash adds to the flavor so leave it on.

▼ Cut the squash into halves. Scrape out and discard the seeds and membranes. Cut the squash into 1-inch pieces.

▼ Place the squash in a steamer basket over boiling water. Steam, covered, for several minutes or until tender. Salt lightly and set aside.

▼ Heat the olive oil and butter in a large skillet over medium-high heat.

▼ Add the garlic. Sauté until the garlic begins to brown.

▼ Add the soy sauce and squash and toss carefully.

▼ Sprinkle with the sesame seeds and serve immediately.

Yield: 4 servings

Fort for Sale

Following the "fort" period for which Fort Clinch is historically known was another period of somewhat unsuccessful property development. Sometime after the federal government sold the fort as surplus property, four partners invested $10,000 in the "Fort Clinch Reservation" and subdivided the property into lots, which did not sell. The determined partners then made another attempt at generating revenue by trying to dismantle the fort to sell the bricks. However, the binding mortar proved to be too tough and that project also died. Unable to pay the $8,000 to $10,000 in accrued taxes, they appealed to Dan Kelly, state legislator from Fernandina, and sold the property to the state in 1936 for $10,000 plus back taxes.

Squash Casserole

This excellent recipe will turn squash haters into squash eaters.

▼ Cook the squash in a small amount of water in a large saucepan until tender. Drain well and set aside.

▼ Sauté the onion in ¼ cup butter in a skillet until tender.

▼ Combine the soup, sour cream and water chestnuts in a large bowl and mix well.

▼ Add the squash, sautéed onion and half the crumbs and mix well. Pour into a buttered baking dish.

▼ Bake at 350 degrees for 30 minutes.

▼ Sprinkle the remaining crumbs over the top. Drizzle with the melted butter.

▼ Bake for 10 minutes longer or until golden brown.

Yield: 4 to 6 servings

1½ **pounds squash, chopped**
1 large onion, sliced
¼ **cup butter or margarine**
1 (10-ounce) can cream of chicken soup
1 cup sour cream
1 (7-ounce) can sliced water chestnuts, drained
1 (8-ounce) package seasoned bread crumbs or stuffing mix
¼ **cup melted butter or margarine**

Squash Patties

▼ Grate the squash and place in a paper-towel-lined colander. Grate the onion finely and add to the squash.

▼ Let the squash and onion drain for 1 hour.

▼ Combine the squash and onion in a bowl. Add the egg, salt and pepper and mix well.

▼ Add enough flour to hold the squash mixture together.

▼ Preheat the oil to about 375 degrees in a large skillet.

▼ Drop the squash mixture by small spoonfuls into the hot oil.

▼ Deep-fry until golden brown. Drain on paper towels.

Yield: 6 servings

3 or 4 medium squash
1 small onion
1 egg, beaten
Salt and pepper to taste
½ **cup (about) flour**
Vegetable oil for deep-frying

Sausage-Stuffed Tomatoes

8 ounces mild bulk sausage
4 large firm tomatoes
**3 tablespoons finely chopped
  celery**
**3 tablespoons finely chopped
  green bell pepper**
½ cup soft bread crumbs
Salt and pepper to taste
½ cup shredded Cheddar cheese
Fresh parsley sprigs

▼ Cook the sausage in a skillet until brown and crumbly, stirring frequently. Drain well and set aside.

▼ Cut the tops from the tomatoes. Scoop out the pulp, leaving the shells intact.

▼ Chop the tomato pulp and place in a bowl.

▼ Add the celery, green pepper and bread crumbs to the tomato pulp and mix well. Mix in the cooked sausage.

▼ Sprinkle the tomato shells with salt and pepper. Place the shells in an 8x8-inch baking pan.

▼ Spoon the sausage mixture into the shells.

▼ Bake at 350 degrees for 15 minutes or until heated through.

▼ Sprinkle with the cheese. Bake for 1 minute longer or until the cheese melts.

▼ Garnish with parsley sprigs.

Yield: 4 servings

Brandied Yams

This recipe is a standing request for all family holiday dinners.

▼ Scrub the yams. Cook in boiling water to cover in a large saucepan until tender. Drain and cool.
▼ Peel the yams and cut into ¼-inch-thick slices.
▼ Butter a large shallow baking dish generously. Layer the yam slices in the baking dish, dotting with 6 tablespoons butter.
▼ Reserve a small amount of the Brandy Sauce for basting.
▼ Spoon the remaining Brandy Sauce over the yam layers, fitting the raisins and apple slices from the Brandy Sauce around and between the yam layers.
▼ Bake at 350 degrees for 30 minutes, basting occasionally with the reserved Brandy Sauce.

4 large yams
6 tablespoons butter or margarine
Brandy Sauce

Brandy Sauce

▼ Dissolve the cornstarch in 1 tablespoon water in a medium saucepan.
▼ Add the brown sugar and ¾ cup water. Add the butter and raisins and mix well.
▼ Bring to a boil, stirring constantly. Cook until thick and glossy, stirring constantly.
▼ Remove from the heat and let stand until partially cooled.
▼ Add the nutmeg, lemon juice and brandy and mix well.
▼ Stir in the apple slices.

   Yield: 16 to 20 servings

1 tablespoon cornstarch
1 tablespoon water
⅔ cup packed brown sugar
¾ cup water
2 tablespoons butter or margarine
¼ cup raisins
½ teaspoon nutmeg
2 tablespoons lemon juice
¼ cup brandy
½ to 1 cup sliced unpeeled green apples

Sweet Potato Casserole

1 (40-ounce) can sweet potatoes
1/4 cup melted margarine
2 eggs
1 cup sugar
2 teaspoons vanilla extract
1/2 cup evaporated milk
Salt to taste
1 cup packed brown sugar
1/2 cup flour
1/4 cup margarine
1/2 cup chopped pecans

▼ Drain the sweet potatoes. Place in a large bowl. Mash or beat until smooth.

▼ Add melted margarine, eggs, sugar, vanilla, evaporated milk and salt and beat until smooth and creamy.

▼ Spoon into a greased baking dish.

▼ Mix the brown sugar and flour in a small bowl. Cut in the margarine until crumbly. Stir in the pecans.

▼ Sprinkle over the sweet potato mixture.

▼ Bake at 350 degrees for 30 minutes.

Yield: 15 servings

Yum-Yum Yams

3 (17-ounce) can yams
1 (6-ounce) can frozen orange
   juice concentrate, thawed
1/2 cup light corn syrup
1/4 cup packed brown sugar
2 tablespoons margarine
Orange slices

▼ Drain the yams well. Arrange the yams in a single layer in a greased 9x13-inch baking dish.

▼ Combine the orange juice concentrate, corn syrup, brown sugar and margarine in a large skillet over medium heat.

▼ Bring to a boil, stirring constantly.

▼ Boil for 10 minutes or until thick and syrupy, stirring frequently.

▼ Spoon over the yams.

▼ Bake at 325 degrees for 20 to 25 minutes or until heated through, basting often.

▼ Spoon into a serving dish. Garnish with the orange slices.

Yield: 12 servings

Mock Crab Cakes

▼ Drain the zucchini well and place on several layers of paper towels. Cover with additional towels and press to remove excess moisture.

▼ Combine the zucchini, eggs, bread crumbs, onion, seasoning and mayonnaise and mix well.

▼ Divide the mixture into 8 portions and shape each portion into a patty. The mixture will be soft.

▼ Pour 1/4 inch oil into a large heavy skillet over medium-high heat.

▼ Add the patties two or three at a time. Fry for 2 minutes on each side or until brown. Drain on paper towels.

Yield: 4 servings

2 cups grated zucchini
2 eggs, slightly beaten
1 cup fine dry bread crumbs
1/2 small onion, chopped
2 to 3 teaspoons Old Bay
 seasoning
1 teaspoon mayonnaise
Vegetable oil for frying

Zucchini-Crust Pizza

▼ Sprinkle the zucchini lightly with salt. Let stand for 15 minutes. Drain and squeeze the zucchini dry.

▼ Mix the zucchini, eggs, flour, mozzarella cheese, Parmesan cheese, basil, salt and pepper in a bowl.

▼ Spread the mixture evenly in an oiled 9x13-inch baking pan.

▼ Bake at 350 degrees for 20 to 25 minutes or until the surface is dry and firm.

▼ Brush the surface with the oil.

▼ Broil for about 5 minutes or until golden brown.

▼ Add your favorite pizza toppings such as sauce, olives, sautéed mushrooms, bell pepper strips and cheese.

▼ Bake for about 25 minutes. Cut into squares and serve hot.

Yield: 4 to 6 servings

3 1/2 cups coarsely grated zucchini
Salt
3 eggs
1/3 cup flour
1/2 cup shredded mozzarella
 cheese
1/2 cup grated Parmesan cheese
1 tablespoon minced fresh basil,
 or 1/2 teaspoon dried
Salt and pepper to taste
1 to 2 tablespoons vegetable oil
Favorite pizza toppings

Granny's Country Dressing

1 sleeve butter crackers, crushed
2 cups crumbled cold corn bread
1 (8-ounce) package herb-
    seasoned stuffing mix
4 slices bread, toasted, crumbled
1 onion, chopped
1/2 cup chopped celery
1/2 cup margarine
1/2 teaspoon celery seeds
Chicken or turkey stock
Salt to taste
1/2 teaspoon pepper

This is a family recipe that dates back over one hundred years. It has been "modernized" by using the butter crackers instead of soda crackers and adding a package of stuffing mix.

▼ Combine the crackers, corn bread, stuffing mix and toast in a large bowl.

▼ Sauté the onion and celery in the margarine in a saucepan until the onion is transparent.

▼ Add the sautéed vegetables to the stuffing mixture and mix well. Add the celery seeds.

▼ Add enough chicken stock to make the mixture moist enough to shape into balls. Add salt and pepper.

▼ Shape into 2 1/2-inch balls and arrange on a greased baking sheet.

▼ Bake at 350 degrees until heated through and lightly toasted.

Yield: 8 servings

Company Macaroni and Cheese

▼ Cook the macaroni according to the package directions. Drain well and set aside.

▼ Combine the soup, milk, pimento, sauce, green onions, parsley flakes and red pepper flakes in a medium bowl and mix well.

▼ Sauté the bread crumbs in the butter in a large skillet until brown. Mix in the seasoned salt and set aside.

▼ Spray a shallow baking dish with nonstick cooking spray.

▼ Layer the macaroni, soup mixture and cheese ½ at a time in the prepared baking dish.

▼ Sprinkle the bread crumbs over the top.

▼ Bake at 350 degrees for 30 to 40 minutes or until bubbly and crusty on top.

Yield: 6 servings

2 cups uncooked elbow macaroni
1 cup Cheddar cheese soup
½ cup milk
1 (2-ounce) jar chopped pimento
1 teaspoon Pickapepper sauce
1 tablespoon (or more) finely chopped green onions
1 tablespoon parsley flakes
2 dashes of red pepper flakes
2 or 3 slices whole wheat bread, crumbled
3 to 4 tablespoons butter
1 or 2 dashes seasoned salt
1½ cups shredded Cheddar cheese

Chinese Fried Rice

This recipe is best with refrigerated leftover rice.

▼ Fry the bacon in a large skillet until crisp. Remove the bacon to paper towels to drain, reserving the pan drippings in the skillet.

▼ Scramble the eggs in a nonstick skillet and set aside.

▼ Add the rice to the bacon drippings in the skillet. Fry until the rice kernels have warmed and separated.

▼ Crumble the bacon into the rice.

▼ Add the scrambled eggs, green onions and soy sauce.

▼ Cook until heated through, stirring and turning constantly.

Yield: 10 servings

8 slices bacon
4 eggs
5 cups cooked rice
4 green onions, chopped
2 to 3 tablespoons soy sauce

That Special Touch

Desserts

Golden Era

Fernandina's greatest era of prosperity to date lasted roughly from the end of Reconstruction to just before World War I. During this period, which has been called the Golden Era (1873–1910), commercial development, a burgeoning tourist industry, and the rise of the middle class brought a surge of population growth and blossoming architectural styles in Fernandina.

Fernandina Beach, called the "Manhattan of the South," was expected to keep pace with Manhattan Island. At one time fourteen foreign consuls officed on Amelia Island. The large, magnificent post office on Centre Street indicates the importance of the town and the growth that was expected to continue.

The steamship lines were bringing people to enjoy the wonderful climate and the excitement of this new place. There were two grand hotels—the Egmont, in town, and the Strathmore, at the beach—with a trolley connecting the two.

The Golden Era ended when Henry Flagler went further south with his railroad and opulent hotels, luring tourist trade to even warmer climes. Modern dredging made other ports attractive and took commerce from the island.

Historic District

The past is visible in downtown Fernandina Beach. The handsome brick blocks on Centre Street and the lovely, old homes north and south of Centre act as reminders that this was a thriving Victorian seaport. The fifty-three-block area of downtown is listed as a Historic District in the National Register because of its uniform concentration of late-Victorian architecture.

The jewels of the Historic District are St. Peter's Episcopal Church, the Nassau County Courthouse, and the Post Office. The sand and oyster-shell streets are long gone, but a walking tour of the Historic District turns back the clock.

Blintz Soufflé with Blueberry Sauce

▼ Combine the cream cheese, cottage cheese, egg yolks, 1 tablespoon sugar and vanilla in a small mixer bowl. Beat at medium speed until smooth and well blended. Set aside.

▼ Combine the eggs, 1½ cups sour cream, orange juice and butter in a blender container and process until smooth.

▼ Add the flour, ¼ cup sugar, baking powder and orange zest and process until smooth.

▼ Pour half the batter into a greased 9x13-inch baking dish.

▼ Spoon the cream cheese mixture evenly over the batter and spread carefully with a knife.

▼ Pour the remaining batter evenly over the top.

▼ Bake at 350 degrees for 50 to 60 minutes or until puffy and golden brown.

▼ Cut into squares and serve immediately with warm Blueberry Sauce and a dollop of sour cream.

8 ounces cream cheese, softened
2 cups small curd cottage cheese
2 egg yolks
1 tablespoon sugar
1 teaspoon vanilla extract
6 eggs
1½ cups sour cream
½ cup orange juice
½ cup butter or margarine, softened
1 cup flour
¼ cup sugar
2 teaspoons baking powder
1 teaspoon grated orange zest
Blueberry Sauce
Sour cream to taste

Blueberry Sauce

▼ Mix the sugar, cornstarch and nutmeg in a heavy saucepan.

▼ Stir in the water gradually. Cook over medium heat until the mixture comes to a boil and thickens, stirring constantly.

▼ Boil for 1 minute, stirring constantly.

▼ Stir in the blueberries and lemon juice. Heat to serving temperature.

Yield: 8 to 10 servings

½ cup sugar
2 tablespoons cornstarch
Nutmeg to taste
1 cup water
2 cups blueberries
2 tablespoons lemon juice

Chocolate Delight

1½ cups flour
¾ cup finely chopped pecans
¾ cup melted butter
8 ounces cream cheese, softened
1 cup confectioners' sugar
12 ounces whipped topping
1 (4-ounce) package vanilla
  instant pudding mix
1 (4-ounce) package chocolate
  instant pudding mix
3 cups milk
Grated chocolate and/or chopped
  pecans to taste

▼ Combine the flour and ¾ cup pecans in a bowl. Add the butter and mix well. Press the mixture over the bottom of a 9x13-inch baking dish.

▼ Bake at 375 degrees for 15 minutes. Let stand until completely cool.

▼ Beat the cream cheese, confectioners' sugar and half the whipped topping in a bowl until well blended. Spread over the cooled crust. Combine the pudding mixes in a bowl. Add the milk gradually. Beat until well blended and thickened. Spread over the cream cheese mixture.

▼ Let stand for several minutes until set. Spread the remaining whipped topping over the top.

▼ Sprinkle with grated chocolate and/or chopped pecans to taste. Chill, covered, until serving time.

Yield: 15 servings

Chocolate Angel Delight

2 cups chocolate chips, melted
3 tablespoons water
½ teaspoon cinnamon
4 egg yolks, beaten
4 egg whites
3 tablespoons sugar
2 cups whipping cream, whipped
½ cup chopped pecans
½ angel food cake

▼ Combine the melted chocolate, water, cinnamon and egg yolks in a large bowl. Blend well and set aside.

▼ Beat the egg whites in a mixer bowl until soft peaks form. Add the sugar gradually, beating until stiff peaks form. Fold the beaten egg whites and whipped cream into the chocolate mixture gently. Fold in the pecans.

▼ Remove the loose crumbs from the surface of the cake. Cut or tear the cake into bite-size pieces. Fold the cake into the chocolate mixture gently.

▼ Spoon the mixture into a serving bowl. Garnish with maraschino cherries, additional pecans or additional whipped cream.

Yield: 8 to 12 servings

Granny's Basic Cake

▼ Combine the oil, sugar and eggs in a mixer bowl. Beat for 10 minutes.
▼ Add the flour alternately with the milk and vanilla, beating well after each addition. Beat for 10 minutes, scraping the side of the bowl occasionally.
▼ Pour the batter into 2 greased and floured 9-inch round cake pans.
▼ Bake at 350 degrees for 25 to 30 minutes or until the layers test done.
▼ Cool in the pans for several minutes.
▼ Invert onto a wire rack to cool completely.
▼ Spread the Easy Cream Cheese Frosting between the layers and over the top and side of the cake.

1 cup vegetable oil
2 cups sugar
4 eggs
2 cups self-rising flour
1 cup milk
1 teaspoon vanilla extract
Easy Cream Cheese Frosting

Easy Cream Cheese Frosting

▼ Beat the cream cheese in a mixer bowl until light.
▼ Add the whipped topping and beat until smooth and creamy.

Yield: 16 servings

8 ounces cream cheese, softened
12 ounces whipped topping

Fourteen-Carrot Cake

2 cups sifted flour
2 teaspoons baking powder
1¹/₂ teaspoons baking soda
1¹/₂ teaspoons salt
2 teaspoons cinnamon
2 cups sugar
1¹/₂ cups vegetable oil
4 eggs
2 cups grated carrots
1 (8-ounce) can crushed
   pineapple
¹/₂ cup chopped pecans (optional)
1 (3-ounce) package flaked
   coconut
Buttery Cream Cheese Frosting

▼ Sift the flour, baking powder, baking soda, salt and cinnamon into a large bowl.
▼ Add the sugar, oil and eggs and beat until well blended.
▼ Stir in the carrots, pineapple, pecans and coconut.
▼ Pour into a greased and floured bundt pan.
▼ Bake at 350 degrees for 55 minutes or until the cake tests done.
▼ Cool in the pan for about 10 minutes.
▼ Invert onto a wire rack or cake plate to cool completely.
▼ Frost with Buttery Cream Cheese Frosting.

Buttery Cream Cheese Frosting

¹/₂ cup butter, softened
3 ounces cream cheese, softened
1 teaspoon vanilla extract
1 (1-pound) package
   confectioners' sugar
2 tablespoons (about) milk

▼ Combine the butter and cream cheese in a medium bowl and beat until well blended. Beat in the vanilla.
▼ Add the confectioners' sugar gradually, beating until smooth and creamy and adding enough milk to make of spreading consistency.

Yield: 16 servings

Buttermilk Chocolate Cake

- ▼ Combine the flour and sugar in a large bowl. Mix well and set aside.
- ▼ Dissolve the baking soda in the buttermilk and set aside.
- ▼ Combine the margarine, baking cocoa and water in a saucepan. Bring to a boil, stirring until well blended.
- ▼ Pour the chocolate mixture into the sugar mixture and stir until well mixed. Add the eggs and mix well.
- ▼ Add the buttermilk mixture and mix well.
- ▼ Pour into a greased and floured 9x13-inch cake pan.
- ▼ Bake at 300 degrees for 35 to 40 minutes or until the cake tests done.
- ▼ Pour the warm Buttermilk Chocolate Frosting over the warm cake and spread to cover the cake.

2 cups flour
2 cups sugar
1 teaspoon baking soda
1/2 cup buttermilk
1 cup margarine
1/4 cup baking cocoa
1 cup water
2 eggs
Buttermilk Chocolate Frosting

Buttermilk Chocolate Frosting

- ▼ Combine the margarine, baking cocoa and buttermilk in a large saucepan. Bring to a boil, stirring until blended. Remove from the heat.
- ▼ Add the confectioners' sugar gradually, mixing until smooth and creamy.
- ▼ Stir in the pecans.

    Yield: 12 to 15 servings

1/2 cup margarine
1/4 cup baking cocoa
6 tablespoons buttermilk
1 (1-pound) package confectioners' sugar
1 cup chopped pecans

Elegant Chocolate Cupcakes

4 ounces semisweet chocolate
1 cup margarine
1 cup chopped pecans
1 3/4 cups sugar
1 cup flour
4 eggs
1 teaspoon vanilla extract
1/2 teaspoon butter flavoring

These cupcakes need no frosting.

▼ Combine the chocolate and margarine in a heavy saucepan. Heat over medium heat until melted, stirring constantly. Remove from the heat. Add the pecans, stirring until well coated.

▼ Combine the sugar, flour, eggs, vanilla and butter flavoring in a bowl. Stir until well mixed but do not beat.

▼ Add the chocolate mixture and mix gently but well.

▼ Spoon the batter into paper-lined muffin cups, filling 3/4 full.

▼ Bake at 325 degrees for 30 minutes.

▼ Do not substitute butter for margarine in this recipe.

Yield: 12 to 15 servings

Historic District Highlights

Fernandina has some of the oldest and finest examples of Florida architecture found anywhere in the state. See examples of Queen Anne, Italianate, and Greek Revival influence, with smaller influences of Gothic Revival, Colonial Vernacular, Italian Renaissance, Colonial Revival, Neoclassical, and Mission styles.

Chocolate Pound Cake

▼ Combine the butter and shortening in a large bowl and beat with an electric mixer at medium speed for about 2 minutes or until creamy.

▼ Add the sugar gradually, beating constantly. Beat for 5 to 7 minutes or until light and fluffy.

▼ Add the eggs 1 at a time, beating after each addition just until the yellow disappears.

▼ Combine the flour, baking cocoa, baking powder and salt and mix well.

▼ Add the flour mixture to the butter mixture alternately with the milk and vanilla, beginning and ending with the flour mixture and beating at low speed after each addition just until blended.

▼ Pour the batter into a greased and floured 10-inch tube pan.

▼ Bake at 325 degrees for 1½ hours or until a wooden pick inserted near the center comes out clean.

▼ Cool in the pan on a wire rack for 10 to 15 minutes.

▼ Invert onto a wire rack to cool completely.

Yield: 16 servings

1 cup butter or margarine, softened
1 cup shortening
3 cups sugar
5 eggs
3 cups flour
¼ cup baking cocoa
½ teaspoon baking powder
½ teaspoon salt
1 cup milk
1 tablespoon vanilla extract

Chocolate Chip Pound Cake

1 (2-layer) package yellow
   pudding-recipe cake mix
1 (4-ounce) package chocolate
   instant pudding mix
½ cup sugar
¾ cup vegetable oil
¾ cup water
4 eggs
1 cup sour cream
1 cup semisweet chocolate chips
2 tablespoons (about)
   confectioners' sugar

▼ Combine the cake mix, pudding mix and sugar in a large bowl. Mix with a wire whisk to remove the large lumps.

▼ Add the oil, water, eggs and sour cream and mix until smooth.

▼ Stir in the chocolate chips.

▼ Pour the batter into a greased and floured 12-cup bundt pan.

▼ Bake at 350 degrees for 1 hour or until a wooden pick inserted near the center comes out clean.

▼ Cool in the pan on a wire rack for about 10 minutes.

▼ Invert onto a wire rack to cool completely.

▼ Sprinkle with the confectioners' sugar.

Yield: 16 servings

Variation: For ***Vanilla Pound Cake***, substitute a yellow cake mix for the yellow pudding-recipe cake mix, vanilla instant pudding mix for the chocolate instant pudding mix, and use 1 cup milk instead of the sour cream and water. Bake and cool as above.

Cranberry Bundt Cake

- ▼ Combine the poppy seeds with water to cover in a small bowl. Let soak for about 10 minutes; drain.
- ▼ Combine the cake mix, pudding mix, oil, eggs and warm water in a large mixer bowl. Beat with an electric mixer for 2 minutes. Beat in the poppy seeds and cranberries.
- ▼ Pour into a greased and floured tube or bundt pan.
- ▼ Bake at 350 degrees for 1 to 1¼ hours or until the cake tests done.
- ▼ Cool in the pan on a wire rack for 10 minutes.
- ▼ Invert onto a wire rack to cool completely.

Yield: 16 servings

⅓ **cup poppy seeds**
1 **(2-layer) package yellow cake mix**
1 **(4-ounce) package vanilla instant pudding mix**
½ **cup vegetable oil**
4 **eggs**
1 **cup warm water**
2 **cups fresh cranberries, rinsed, drained**

Wedding Gifts

Three of Fernandina's most beautiful Victorian-era homes were built as wedding gifts. In 1885, *Fernandina Mirror* editor and Florida historian Major George R. Fairbanks commissioned architect Robert Sands Schuyler to build an Italianate mansion on the corner of South 7th and Cedar Streets as a surprise for his second wife, a shy young lass from rural Tennessee. In 1895, Effingham Bailey, a steamship agent for the Mallory Line and investor in the trolley which was to branch out along South 7th Street on its way from the river front to the Atlantic, spent the incredible sum of ten thousand dollars to build a beautiful George Barber-designed Queen Anne house for his bride Kate, whose father had donated the building lot on the corner of South 7th and Ash Streets to the newlyweds. The Fairbanks House and the Bailey House, listed on the National Register of Historic Places, today operate as bed and breakfast inns. The final wedding-gift house, which remains a private residence to this day, is the Villa Las Palmas at 315 Alachua Street. Built in 1910 by the fifty-two-year-old businessman/ adventurer Colonel "Honey" Borden for his beautiful seventeen-year-old bride Flossie, this striking home is an architectural hybrid conceived by local builder John Mann, who mixed Mediterranean, Colonial Revival, and Art Nouveau styles to create this impressive home.

Cream Cheese Cake

1/2 cup margarine, softened
1 cup shortening
2 cups sugar
5 egg yolks
1 cup buttermilk
1 1/2 teaspoons salt
1 teaspoon baking soda
1 teaspoon vanilla extract
2 cups flour
1 (3-ounce) can flaked coconut
1 cup chopped pecans
5 egg whites, stiffly beaten
Cream Cheese Frosting

Brett's Waterway Cafe, located on the water at the foot of Centre Street, provides a dining experience you won't want to miss. Brett recommends his Cream Cheese Cake recipe for special occasions and holidays. Try surrounding this cake with fresh berries and fruits of the season.

▼ Cream the margarine, shortening and sugar in a large bowl until light and fluffy.
▼ Add the egg yolks 1 at a time, beating well after each addition.
▼ Combine the buttermilk, salt, baking soda and vanilla in a small bowl and mix well.
▼ Add the buttermilk mixture alternately with the flour to the creamed mixture, mixing well after each addition.
▼ Fold in the coconut, pecans and egg whites. Pour into 3 greased and floured 9-inch cake pans.
▼ Bake at 350 degrees for 25 to 30 minutes or until the layers test done.
▼ Cool in the pans on a wire rack for 10 minutes.
▼ Invert onto a wire rack to cool completely.
▼ Spread the Cream Cheese Frosting between the layers and over the top and side of the cake.

Cream Cheese Frosting

8 ounces cream cheese, softened
1/2 cup margarine, softened
1 teaspoon vanilla extract
1 (1-pound) package
 confectioners' sugar

▼ Combine the cream cheese, margarine and vanilla in a bowl and beat until well blended.
▼ Add the confectioners' sugar gradually, beating after each addition until smooth and creamy.

Yield: 16 servings

Hummingbird Cake

This cake gets its name from the sound you make when you taste it—"Hummmmm."

▼ Combine the flour, sugar, baking soda, cinnamon and salt in a large bowl and mix well.
▼ Add the eggs and oil and stir until well mixed; do not beat.
▼ Add the vanilla, undrained pineapple, bananas and pecans and mix well.
▼ Pour into three 9-inch cake pans sprayed with nonstick cooking spray.
▼ Bake at 350 degrees for 25 minutes or until the layers test done.
▼ Cool in the pans on wire racks for 10 minutes.
▼ Remove from the pans to wire racks to cool completely.
▼ Spread Cream Cheese Pecan Frosting between the layers and over the top and side of the cake.

3 cups flour
2 cups sugar
1 teaspoon baking soda
1 teaspoon cinnamon
$1/2$ teaspoon salt
3 eggs, beaten
$3/4$ cup vegetable oil
$1 1/2$ teaspoons vanilla extract
1 (8-ounce) can crushed pineapple
3 bananas, mashed
1 cup chopped pecans
Cream Cheese Pecan Frosting

Cream Cheese Pecan Frosting

▼ Combine the butter and cream cheese in a medium mixer bowl and beat at low speed until well blended. Beat in the vanilla.
▼ Add the confectioners' sugar gradually, beating until smooth and creamy.
▼ Add the pecans and stir until well mixed.

Yield: 16 servings

$1/2$ cup butter, softened
8 ounces cream cheese, softened
1 teaspoon vanilla extract
1 (1-pound) package confectioners' sugar
$1/2$ cup chopped pecans

Mother Floyd's Orange Christmas Cake

1 (2-layer) package orange cake
  mix
1 (3-ounce) package orange
  gelatin
½ cup vegetable oil
1½ cups water
2 eggs
Orange Coconut Filling
Orange Coconut Frosting

▼ Combine the cake mix, gelatin, oil, water and eggs in a large bowl. Beat for 2 minutes or until well blended.

▼ Pour the batter into 3 greased and floured 9-inch cake pans.

▼ Bake at 350 degrees for 25 to 30 minutes or until the layers test done.

▼ Cool in the pans on a wire rack for 10 minutes.

▼ Invert onto a wire rack to cool completely.

▼ Spread the Orange Coconut Filling between the layers.

▼ Spread the Orange Coconut Frosting over the top and side of the cake.

▼ Refrigerate the cake for 2 days before serving.

Orange Coconut Filling

¾ cup sour cream
1 (2-ounce) package frozen flaked
  coconut
½ cup orange juice
1¼ cups sugar

▼ Combine the sour cream, coconut, orange juice and sugar in a medium bowl and mix well.

▼ Reserve 1 cup of the mixture for the frosting.

Orange Coconut Frosting

1 cup Orange Coconut Filling
9 ounces whipped topping

▼ Combine the Orange Coconut Filling with the whipped topping in a bowl and mix well.

Yield: 16 servings

Praline Cake

▼ Combine the brown sugar, butter and cream in a saucepan. Cook over low heat until the butter melts and the mixture is smooth and well mixed, stirring constantly.

▼ Pour into 2 ungreased 9-inch cake pans. Sprinkle with the roasted almonds. Set the cake pans aside.

▼ Combine the cake mix, buttermilk, vanilla and almond flavorings, lemon zest, eggs, oil and nutmeg in a large mixer bowl. Beat with an electric mixer at low speed for 2 minutes.

▼ Spoon the batter into the prepared cake pans.

▼ Bake at 325 degrees for 20 to 25 minutes or until the layers test done.

▼ Cool in the pans on a wire rack for 5 to 8 minutes.

▼ Invert onto a wire rack to cool completely.

▼ Spread the whipped topping between the layers and over the top. Do not frost the side.

▼ Sprinkle the ground almonds over the top. May top with nut halves instead of ground nuts.

▼ Chill in the refrigerator before serving. Prepare the cake a day ahead for better flavor.

Yield: 16 servings

1 cup packed brown sugar
$1/2$ cup butter
$1/4$ cup cream
1 cup chopped almonds, walnuts or pecans, roasted
1 (2-layer) package yellow cake mix
1 cup buttermilk
1 teaspoon vanilla extract
1 teaspoon almond extract
Grated zest of 1 lemon
3 eggs
$1/3$ cup vegetable oil
1 teaspoon nutmeg
16 ounces whipped topping
Ground almonds, walnuts or pecans

Coconut Cream Cheesecake

2 cups graham cracker crumbs
3 tablespoons sugar
1/2 cup melted butter or margarine
24 ounces cream cheese, softened
1 cup whipping cream
1 1/2 cups sugar
1 teaspoon lemon juice
4 eggs
2 egg yolks
2 1/2 cups (about) flaked coconut

▼ Combine the graham cracker crumbs, 3 tablespoons sugar and melted butter in a bowl and mix well.

▼ Press the mixture over the bottom and 1/3 of the way up the side of a greased 9- or 10-inch springform pan. Set the pan aside.

▼ Combine the cream cheese and whipping cream in a bowl and beat until smooth.

▼ Add the sugar, lemon juice, eggs and egg yolks and beat until well blended.

▼ Add 2 cups of the coconut and mix well.

▼ Pour the mixture into the prepared springform pan.

▼ Bake at 325 degrees for 1 1/2 hours or until firm and golden brown.

▼ Let stand to cool completely.

▼ Refrigerate until serving time.

▼ Spread the remaining 1/2 cup coconut on a baking sheet.

▼ Bake at 325 degrees for 7 to 10 minutes or until toasted to a golden brown, stirring occasionally. Cool completely.

▼ Loosen the cheesecake from the side of the pan. Remove the side of the pan.

▼ Sprinkle the toasted coconut over the top of the cheesecake.

Yield: 10 to 12 servings

Frozen Mocha Cheesecake

▼ Combine the cookie crumbs, sugar and melted margarine in a bowl and mix well.

▼ Pat the crumb mixture over the bottom and up the sides of a buttered 9x13-inch dish.

▼ Chill until the crust is firm.

▼ Beat the cream cheese in a large mixer bowl until fluffy. Add the condensed milk and the chocolate syrup and beat until smooth and creamy.

▼ Dissolve the coffee powder in the hot water. Add to the cream cheese mixture and mix well.

▼ Fold in the whipped cream gently.

▼ Pour the cream cheese mixture into the prepared dish.

▼ Freeze, covered, for 6 hours or until firm.

▼ Store the cheesecake, covered, in the freezer.

Yield: 14 to 16 servings

1¼ **cups chocolate wafer cookie crumbs**
¼ **cup sugar**
¼ **cup melted margarine**
8 ounces cream cheese, softened
1 (14-ounce) can sweetened condensed milk
⅔ **cup chocolate syrup**
2 tablespoons instant coffee powder
1 teaspoon hot water
1 cup whipping cream, whipped

Mrs. Bailey's Tree

Just south of the gracious veranda on Ash Street stands "Mrs. Bailey's Tree"—so named because she sat on her porch, shotgun in hand, and dared any city worker to cut down the tree when the street was being paved. This is why the magnificent old oak remains, and Ash Street curves around it.

Heather's Oreo Cheesecake

18 to 20 Oreo cookies
32 ounces cream cheese, softened
1⅓ cups sugar
1½ teaspoons vanilla extract
2 teaspoons cornstarch
4 eggs
½ cup whipping cream

▼ Preheat the oven to 350 degrees.

▼ Butter an 8-inch springform pan. Stand 12 of the cookies on edge around the side of the pan.

▼ Cut the remaining cookies into fourths and set aside.

▼ Beat the cream cheese in a large mixer bowl with an electric mixer at medium speed until light and fluffy.

▼ Add the sugar gradually, beating constantly. Beat in the vanilla and cornstarch.

▼ Add the eggs 1 at a time, beating well after each addition.

▼ Stir in the cream and blend well.

▼ Spoon about ¼ of the cream cheese mixture into the prepared pan. Sprinkle with about ⅓ of the cookie pieces.

▼ Alternate layers of the remaining cream cheese mixture and cookie pieces, ending with the cream cheese mixture.

▼ Wrap the bottom and side of the pan with heavy-duty foil to prevent leaking. Place the springform pan in a large pan.

▼ Place the large pan on the oven rack. Add hot water to the large pan to a depth of 1½ inches.

▼ Bake for 1 hour. Turn off the oven.

▼ Let the cheesecake stand in the closed oven for 1 hour.

▼ Remove the springform pan to a wire rack to cool.

▼ Refrigerate the cheesecake, covered, for several hours.

▼ Loosen the cheesecake from the side of the pan. Remove the side of the pan.

Yield: 16 servings

Peaches and Cream Cheesecake

▼ Combine the flour, pudding mix, salt, margarine, egg and milk in a medium bowl and beat until well mixed.

▼ Pat the mixture into a greased pie plate.

▼ Drain the peaches, reserving 3 tablespoons of the juice.

▼ Arrange the peach slices in the prepared pie plate.

▼ Combine the cream cheese, ½ cup sugar and reserved peach juice in a bowl and beat until well blended. Spoon over the peaches.

▼ Mix the cinnamon with 1 tablespoon sugar. Sprinkle over the cream cheese mixture.

▼ Bake at 350 degrees for 30 minutes or until set.

▼ Let stand until cool.

▼ Chill, covered, in the refrigerator.

Yield: 8 to 10 servings

¾ cup flour
1 (4-ounce) package vanilla instant pudding mix
½ teaspoon salt
3 tablespoons margarine
1 egg
½ cup milk
1 (28-ounce) can sliced peaches
8 ounces cream cheese, softened
½ cup sugar
½ teaspoon cinnamon
1 tablespoon sugar

Chocolate Raspberry Truffles

1$^1\!/_3$ **cups semisweet chocolate chips**
2 **tablespoons whipping cream**
1 **tablespoon butter**
2 **tablespoons seedless raspberry jam**
6 **ounces white chocolate or milk chocolate**
2 **teaspoons shortening**

▼ Combine the chocolate chips, cream and butter in a heavy saucepan. Cook over low heat until smooth, stirring constantly. Stir in the jam.

▼ Remove from the heat. Cover with plastic wrap. Freeze for 20 minutes.

▼ Drop by teaspoonfuls onto a foil-lined cookie sheet. Freeze for 15 minutes.

▼ Shape into smooth balls and freeze until firm.

▼ Melt the white chocolate and shortening in a double boiler over hot but not boiling water, stirring constantly until smooth.

▼ Drop the frozen truffles 1 at a time into the melted chocolate; stir quickly to coat and remove with a fork, shaking off the excess chocolate.

▼ Place the coated truffles on a foil-lined cookie sheet.

▼ Chill until set. Store in the refrigerator.

Yield: 48 truffles

Variation: Omit the chocolate coating and roll the frozen truffles in confectioners' sugar or baking cocoa to coat.

Fudge

▼ Combine the evaporated milk, sugar, butter and salt in a large heavy saucepan.

▼ Bring to a boil, stirring constantly. Boil for 5 minutes over medium heat, stirring constantly. Remove from the heat.

▼ Add the marshmallows and chocolate chips. Beat with an electric mixer at medium speed for 2 minutes or until the marshmallows and chocolate chips melt and the mixture is smooth. Beat in the vanilla.

▼ Pour the fudge into a lightly oiled 8x12-inch dish and spread evenly.

▼ Let stand until cool. Cut into squares.

Yield: 60 pieces

Variation: Add peanut butter or chopped nuts to taste to the fudge before pouring into the dish.

2 (5-ounce) cans evaporated milk
3¹/₃ cups sugar
¹/₄ cup butter
Pinch of salt
3 cups miniature marshmallows
3 cups chocolate chips
1 teaspoon vanilla extract

Peanut Brittle

▼ Combine the sugar, water, corn syrup and peanuts in a large heavy saucepan over medium to medium-high heat.

▼ Cook until the peanuts start to pop. Add the baking soda.

▼ Stir until the mixture becomes difficult to stir.

▼ Pour onto a greased baking sheet and spread as thin as possible.

▼ Let stand until cool. Break into pieces.

▼ Store the peanut brittle in an airtight container.

Yield: 10 to 15 servings

1¹/₂ cups sugar
¹/₂ cup water
¹/₃ cup light corn syrup
1¹/₃ cups raw peanuts
1¹/₂ teaspoons baking soda

Lenten Almond Biscotti

2²/₃ cups unblanched almonds
¹/₄ cup sugar
2 cups flour
³/₄ cup sugar
1 cup packed light brown sugar
1 teaspoon cinnamon
1 teaspoon baking powder
3 tablespoons unsalted butter,
   softened
2 eggs, lightly beaten
2 tablespoons milk
1 egg

▼ Spread the almonds in a single layer in a shallow baking pan.

▼ Bake the almonds at 375 degrees for 10 minutes or until toasted, stirring occasionally. Let stand until cool.

▼ Combine about ¹/₄ of the almonds with ¹/₄ cup sugar in a blender container. Process until the almonds are finely ground. Pour into a large bowl.

▼ Chop the remaining almonds coarsely and set aside.

▼ Add the flour, remaining ³/₄ cup sugar, brown sugar, cinnamon and baking powder to the ground almonds and mix well.

▼ Add the butter and mix well.

▼ Add the coarsely chopped almonds and 2 eggs. Mix until the mixture forms a dough.

▼ Divide the dough into 2 equal portions. Shape each portion with floured hands into a 4x15-inch strip. Use spatulas to place the strips on buttered and floured cookie sheets.

▼ Beat the milk with the remaining egg to make an egg wash. Brush the strips with egg wash.

▼ Place the cookie sheets in the upper one-third of a preheated 375-degree oven.

▼ Bake for 20 to 25 minutes or until golden brown and a skewer inserted in the center comes out clean. Turn off the oven.

▼ Cut the rectangles crosswise into ³/₄-inch-thick slices. Return the cookie sheets to the oven.

▼ Let the cookies stand in the closed oven for 15 minutes.

▼ Remove from the oven and let cool completely.

▼ Store the cookies in an airtight container.

Yield: 36 cookies

Tiny's Brownies

Everyone in Fernandina Beach has heard of or eaten Tiny Lewellen's brownies.

▼ Place the sugar in a medium bowl. Add the butter and mix until creamy.
▼ Add the baking cocoa and mix well.
▼ Add the eggs 1 at a time, mixing well after each addition.
▼ Add the flour and mix until smooth. Stir in the vanilla and pecans.
▼ Spread the batter in a greased 10x15-inch baking pan.
▼ Bake at 350 degrees for 25 minutes or until the brownies pull from the sides of the pan.
▼ Let stand until cool.
▼ Pour the hot Brownie Frosting over the cooled brownies. Let stand until the frosting is firm. Cut into squares.

2 cups sugar
1 cup melted butter
$1/4$ cup baking cocoa
4 eggs
$1^{1}/2$ cups sifted flour
1 tablespoon vanilla extract
1 cup pecans or walnuts
Brownie Frosting

Brownie Frosting

▼ Mix the sugar and baking cocoa in a medium saucepan.
▼ Stir in the milk gradually. Add the butter.
▼ Bring to a full rolling boil, stirring constantly. Boil for 1 minute.
▼ Remove from the heat. Add the vanilla.
▼ Beat until the frosting begins to thicken.

Yield: 36 to 48 brownies

2 cups sugar
$1/2$ cup baking cocoa
$1/2$ cup milk
$1/2$ cup butter
1 tablespoon vanilla extract

Cream Cheese Cookies

¹/₂ **cup packed brown sugar**
¹/₄ **cup margarine, softened**
1 cup baking mix
¹/₂ **cup chopped walnuts**
8 ounces cream cheese, softened
¹/₄ **cup sugar**
1 tablespoon lemon juice
2 teaspoons milk
¹/₂ **teaspoon vanilla extract**
1 egg

This recipe is easily doubled and baked in an 11x13-inch pan. The cookies are especially good for the holidays.

▼ Combine the brown sugar and margarine in a bowl and beat until light and fluffy.

▼ Add the baking mix and walnuts and mix until the mixture is crumbly. Reserve 1 cup of the mixture.

▼ Press the remaining mixture in a greased 8x8-inch baking pan.

▼ Bake at 350 degrees for 12 minutes.

▼ Combine the cream cheese and sugar in a mixer bowl and beat until smooth and creamy. Add the lemon juice, milk, vanilla and egg and beat until smooth.

▼ Spread the cream cheese mixture over the baked layer. Sprinkle with the reserved crumb mixture.

▼ Bake for 25 minutes or until the center is firm. Cool on a wire rack.

▼ Cut into 2-inch squares. Store, covered, in the refrigerator.

Yield: 16 cookies

Orange Oatmeal Raisin Cookies

These cookies are absolutely addictive!

- ▼ Combine the raisins and orange juice in a small bowl. Let stand overnight.
- ▼ Cream the butter and sugar in a large bowl until light and fluffy. Beat in the egg and orange zest.
- ▼ Mix the flour and baking soda together. Add to the creamed mixture and mix well.
- ▼ Add the raisins and orange juice, oats and white chocolate chips and mix well.
- ▼ Drop by rounded teaspoonfuls 2 inches apart onto a greased cookie sheet. Flatten slightly.
- ▼ Bake at 350 degrees for 6 minutes. Turn the cookie sheet around. Bake for 4 to 6 minutes longer or until the cookies are golden brown.
- ▼ Cool on the cookie sheet for 1 minute and remove to a wire rack to cool completely.

Yield: 36 cookies

¾ **cup raisins**
3 **tablespoons orange juice**
½ **cup butter, softened**
¾ **cup sugar**
1 **egg**
2 **teaspoons grated orange zest**
1 **cup flour**
1 **teaspoon baking soda**
1½ **cups rolled oats**
1½ **cups white chocolate chips**

Great Pumpkin Cookies

2 cups flour
1 cup quick-cooking oats
1 teaspoon baking soda
1 teaspoon ground cinnamon
1/2 teaspoon salt
1 cup butter or margarine,
 softened
1 cup packed brown sugar
1 cup sugar
1 egg, lightly beaten
1 teaspoon vanilla extract
1 cup pumpkin purée
1 cup semisweet chocolate chips
 or raisins

▼ Combine the flour, oats, baking soda, cinnamon and salt in a bowl. Mix well and set aside.

▼ Cream the butter in a large bowl. Add the brown sugar and sugar gradually, beating constantly until light and fluffy. Beat in the egg and vanilla.

▼ Add the dry ingredients alternately with the pumpkin, mixing well after each addition. Stir in the chocolate chips.

▼ Drop the dough by 1/4 cupfuls onto a lightly greased cookie sheet.

▼ Spread into pumpkin shapes with a thin metal spatula. Add a bit of dough to make stems.

▼ Bake at 350 degrees for 20 to 25 minutes or until the cookies are firm and light brown.

▼ Cool on the cookie sheet for 1 minute. Remove to a wire rack to cool completely.

▼ Decorate as desired.

Yield: 20 cookies

Variation: Drop the dough by teaspoonfuls onto the cookie sheet and bake for 12 minutes or until light brown.

Grandma's Sugar Cookies

- ▼ Blend the margarine and butter in a large mixer bowl.
- ▼ Add 1½ cups sugar gradually, beating until light and fluffy. Beat in the eggs and vanilla.
- ▼ Sift the flour, cream of tartar, baking soda and salt together. Add to the creamed mixture and mix well.
- ▼ Chill the dough, covered, for 2 hours or longer.
- ▼ Shape the dough into walnut-size balls. Dip the tops in sugar. Place sugar side up on an ungreased cookie sheet.
- ▼ Bake at 400 degrees for 8 minutes or until golden brown.
- ▼ Cool on the cookie sheet for 1 minute and remove to a wire rack to cool completely.

Yield: 72 cookies

½ **cup margarine, softened**
½ **cup butter, softened**
1½ **cups sugar**
2 **eggs**
½ **teaspoon vanilla extract**
2¾ **cups flour**
2 **teaspoons cream of tartar**
1 **teaspoon baking soda**
½ **teaspoon salt**
Sugar

Justice Will Be Served

In 1844, Henry Whipple, a young man from western New York, spent the winter in northeast Florida and coastal Georgia as he tried to recover his health. He kept a diary in which he described his observations on the people and places he visited. A religious Presbyterian, he was shocked to learn during his visit to St. Marys that bloody duels were common. To avoid problems with their respective states, Georgians fought their duels on Amelia Island, and Floridians fought their duels on Cumberland Island.

Mr. Whipple saw another form of Florida justice at a session of Nassau County Court, whose county seat had been moved inland from Amelia Island. Court was held in a rude log-and-board building about twelve miles into pine woods. Whipple noted that judges were usually fine men, but the jury was another story. Manslaughter, bigamy, and false packing of cotton all came under the same legal heading. Punishment of murder, when punished at all, was usually two years imprisonment or a $1,000 fine. Mr. Whipple told of one case where a man had stolen a broadaxe. The jury returned a verdict of murder in the first degree. The judge could not accept such a verdict, so he sent the jury back for more deliberations, whereupon the jury told the judge they were sorry, but that was the only verdict they could come up with!

Swedish Apple Pie

2 to 4 Winesap apples, peeled,
   cored, sliced
2 tablespoons flour
3/4 cup sugar
Pinch of salt
1 egg
1 teaspoon vanilla extract
1 cup sour cream
1 unbaked (9-inch) pie shell
1/3 cup flour
1/3 cup sugar
1 teaspoon cinnamon
1/4 cup butter, softened

▼ Cook the apples with a small amount of water in a saucepan until tender. Cool slightly.
▼ Measure 2 cups of the cooked apple slices into a bowl and mash lightly. Reserve any remaining apple slices for another purpose.
▼ Add 2 tablespoons flour, 3/4 cup sugar and salt to the apples and mix well.
▼ Beat the egg with the vanilla. Stir the mixture into the apples. Beat the sour cream in a mixer bowl until stiff. Fold into the apples. Pour the apple mixture into the pie shell.
▼ Bake at 350 degrees for 40 minutes.
▼ Combine 1/3 cup flour, 1/3 cup sugar, cinnamon and butter in a small bowl. Mix with a fork until crumbly.
▼ Sprinkle the cinnamon mixture over the top of the partially baked pie.
▼ Bake for 15 minutes longer or until golden brown.

Yield: 8 to 10 servings

Langford Pecan Pie

2 eggs
1/2 cup sugar
1 cup light corn syrup
1/4 cup melted margarine
2 tablespoons flour
1 teaspoon vanilla extract
1 cup pecan halves
1 unbaked (9-inch) pie shell

▼ Beat the eggs in a large bowl. Add the sugar, corn syrup, margarine, flour and vanilla and mix well.
▼ Stir in the pecan halves.
▼ Pour the mixture into the pie shell.
▼ Bake at 375 degrees for 30 to 60 minutes or until set.
▼ Cool on a wire rack.

Yield: 6 to 8 servings

Fruit Pizza

Use your own favorite fruits. This is especially good when fresh seasonal fruits, such as blueberries and peaches, are used instead of canned fruits.

▼ Cut the cookie dough into ⅛-inch-thick slices and arrange in a pizza pan, pressing the edges together.

▼ Bake according to the package directions until light brown. Place the pizza pan on a wire rack to cool.

▼ Combine the cream cheese, sugar and vanilla in a bowl and beat until smooth and creamy.

▼ Spread the cream cheese mixture over the cooled cookie layer.

▼ Drain the mandarin oranges and pineapple chunks well. Slice the banana. Rinse the strawberries, remove the tops and slice.

▼ Arrange the mandarin oranges, pineapple, banana and strawberries over the cream cheese layer and press in lightly to secure.

▼ Blend the orange marmalade with the lemon juice in a small bowl and brush over the fruit.

▼ Chill the pizza, covered, in the refrigerator until serving time.

▼ Cut into serving pieces. Store any uneaten pizza in the refrigerator.

Yield: 12 to 20 servings

1 (20-ounce) package refrigerated cookie dough
12 ounces cream cheese, softened
½ cup sugar
1½ teaspoons vanilla extract
1 (11-ounce) can mandarin oranges
1 (8-ounce) can pineapple chunks
1 large banana
1 pint fresh strawberries
½ cup orange marmalade
1 teaspoon lemon juice

On the Fast Tract

Easy Recipes

David Levy Yulee and the Florida Railroad

David Levy Yulee was born in 1810 in St. Thomas, Virgin Islands, but became a man of vision for this area. He moved to St. Augustine in 1831, read for the law, was admitted to the bar in 1832, and became involved in politics. Yulee became Territorial Delegate in 1841 and he is credited for getting Florida admitted to the Union in 1845. He was the first elected Jewish senator, but he converted to Christianity in 1846.

In addition to his active political career, Yulee was the founder of the Florida Railroad. In that capacity he had tremendous influence on what happened in Fernandina. His vision was to build a railroad that would run from Fernandina to Cedar Key, 151 miles away on the West Coast of Florida. Goods and materials coming here by ship could be loaded on rail cars and sent across the state to Cedar Key, then reloaded on ships to service the Gulf Coast.

The original town on Amelia Island was Old Town, about two miles across the marsh north of the present town of Fernandina Beach. Yulee convinced the citizens to move the town to the present location for the betterment of the railroad. Work began on the railroad in 1855 and was completed in March 1861, but Yulee's dream was sidetracked because the War Between the States began in April 1861.

After the war, Yulee was imprisoned at Fort Pulaski for ten months because of his secessionist leanings but was able to direct the rebuilding of the Florida Railroad from there. In 1866, Florida's Internal Improvement Board confiscated the railroad for failure to make annual payments.

Easy Minestrone

- ▼ Brown the ground beef in a large heavy stockpot, stirring until crumbly.
- ▼ Add the celery, carrots and onion. Cook until tender, stirring frequently.
- ▼ Add the broth, basil, oregano and pepper. Simmer, covered, for 30 minutes.
- ▼ Add the pasta and spinach. Simmer until the pasta is tender.
- ▼ Add the chick-peas and cheese.
- ▼ Heat to serving temperature. Adjust the seasonings.
- ▼ Serve with additional Parmesan cheese.

Yield: 6 servings

1 pound ground beef
1 cup chopped celery
2 carrots, cut into strips
1/2 cup chopped onion
2 quarts beef broth
1/2 teaspoon chopped basil leaves
1/2 teaspoon chopped oregano leaves
1/4 teaspoon pepper
1 cup tubettini
1 (10-ounce) package frozen chopped spinach
1 (20-ounce) can chick-peas
1 tablespoon Parmesan cheese

Delicious Pork Chops and Rice with Gravy

- ▼ Score the outer edge of the pork chops at 1/2-inch intervals, being careful not to cut into the meat. Season the chops as desired.
- ▼ Preheat a large heavy skillet over medium to medium-high heat. Arrange the chops in the skillet. Cook until cooked through and brown, turning as necessary. Remove the chops from the skillet. Add the soup.
- ▼ Heat the soup to serving temperature, stirring to deglaze the skillet and adding a small amount of water to make gravy of the desired consistency.
- ▼ Place the chops in the gravy. Simmer for 10 minutes or until the chops are tender. Serve the chops and gravy over the hot rice.

Yield: 3 to 4 servings

6 to 8 pork chops
Salt and pepper to taste
2 (10-ounce) cans chicken and rice soup
3 to 4 servings hot cooked rice

Chicken and Rice

**1 (10-ounce) can cream of
  mushroom soup**
1 (10-ounce) can onion soup
2 cups uncooked rice
1 (3-pound) chicken, cut up
Salt and pepper to taste
½ cup butter

▼ Combine the mushroom soup and onion soup in a 4-cup measure. Add enough water to measure 4 cups. Mix well and set aside.

▼ Spread the rice in an even layer in a greased 9x13-inch baking pan.

▼ Rinse the chicken and pat dry.

▼ Season the chicken with salt and pepper and arrange over the rice.

▼ Pour the soup mixture over the chicken and rice.

▼ Dot with the butter.

▼ Bake, covered, at 350 degrees for 45 to 60 minutes or until the rice is tender and the chicken is cooked through.

Yield: 8 to 10 servings

Presidential Visit

Ulysses S. Grant visited Fernandina in 1880 on the steamship *City of Bridgeton*. The former president stopped at the Egmont Hotel to attend a ball on his way to Key West, the West Indies and Mexico. To the surprise of many resident Republicans, Grant was warmly received by ex-Confederates, no doubt due to the fact that he had obtained Senator David Yulee's release from Fort Pulaski after the War Between the States. David Yulee, who was prospering once more with his railroad interests, met with Grant and later asked one of his ex-slaves what he thought of the former president. According to contemporary reports, the old man replied, "Wal, Mr. Yulee, he ain't as hearty a man as yo' Pa."

Easy Chicken

Try this easy method on pork chops, too, adding 1 to 2 teaspoons of prepared mustard to the ketchup mixture.

▼ Rinse the chicken and pat dry. Season with salt and pepper.

▼ Brown the chicken on all sides in the margarine in a large skillet.

▼ Blend the cola and ketchup in a small bowl. Pour half the mixture over the chicken.

▼ Simmer, covered, for 20 minutes.

▼ Add the remaining ketchup mixture. Simmer, covered, for 20 minutes longer or until the chicken is cooked through.

Yield: 4 to 6 servings

1 (3-pound) chicken, cut up
Salt and pepper to taste
1/4 cup margarine
1/2 cup cola
1/2 cup ketchup

Speedy Deep-Dish Pizza

▼ Prepare the pizza dough according to the package directions, using a 9x13-inch baking pan.

▼ Brown the sausage in a skillet, stirring until crumbly; drain well.

▼ Spread the pizza sauce from the mix over the dough.

▼ Add layers of the sausage, onion, green pepper, mozzarella cheese and Cheddar cheese.

▼ Top with the pepperoni and mushrooms. Sprinkle with the Parmesan cheese from the mix.

▼ Bake at 350 degrees for 30 minutes.

▼ Vary toppings as desired.

Yield: 8 servings

1 (16-ounce) package pizza mix
1 pound bulk sausage
1 onion, chopped
1 green bell pepper, chopped
1 (8-ounce) package shredded
  mozzarella cheese
1 (8-ounce) package shredded
  Cheddar cheese
1 (3-ounce) package sliced
  pepperoni
1 (4-ounce) jar sliced mushrooms,
  drained

Impossible Vegetable Pie

1 bunch fresh broccoli, coarsely
 chopped
½ cup chopped onion
½ cup chopped green bell pepper
Salt to taste
1 cup boiling water
2 cups shredded Cheddar cheese
3 eggs
1½ cups milk
¾ cup baking mix
1 teaspoon salt
¼ teaspoon pepper

▼ Cook the broccoli, onion and green pepper in lightly salted boiling water for 5 minutes or until tender-crisp. Drain well.

▼ Spread the vegetables in a lightly greased 10-inch pie plate. Sprinkle with the cheese.

▼ Beat the eggs in a medium bowl. Add the milk, baking mix, 1 teaspoon salt and pepper and beat until well blended.

▼ Pour the egg mixture over the vegetables and cheese.

▼ Bake at 400 degrees for 35 to 40 minutes or until puffed and golden brown.

▼ Let stand for 5 to 10 minutes before cutting.

Yield: 8 to 10 servings

First Island Bowling Alley

In 1877 the Florida Railroad Company constructed the Egmont Hotel, a seventy-five-room resort that covered more than half a block on the west side of South 7th Street. Across 7th Street from the hotel was a beautifully landscaped park. Although the hotel developers had tried to buy the entire block, they could not convince the adjoining Northern Colored Methodist Church to sell to them—and for a very good reason. The northern visitors to the hotel were very generous in making contributions to the church. Church services, characterized by lots of singing and preaching, lasted far into the night to the annoyance of hotel guests. The hotel managers decided to fight fire with fire and erected a bowling alley adjacent to the church. For several weeks neighbors and guests were treated to the nightly sounds of crashing pins and shouting church goers. Finally, the church gave up and moved to another location.

Vidalia Onion Quiche

- ▼ Place the onions in the pie shell.
- ▼ Pour the quiche filling over the onions.
- ▼ Bake according to the package directions.
- ▼ Let stand for 5 minutes before cutting.

Yield: 6 servings

2 cups sliced or chopped Vidalia
  onions
1 unbaked (9-inch) pie shell
1 carton frozen cheese quiche
  filling, thawed

Cheese Mini-Muffins

- ▼ Beat the margarine in a large bowl.
- ▼ Add the sour cream and mix well.
- ▼ Add the flour gradually, mixing well after each addition.
- ▼ Mix in the cheese.
- ▼ Drop the dough by teaspoonfuls into greased miniature muffin cups.
- ▼ Bake at 400 degrees for 20 minutes or until golden brown.
- ▼ Remove from the cups immediately.

Yield: 36 miniature muffins

1 cup margarine, softened
1 cup sour cream
2 cups self-rising flour
1 cup shredded sharp Cheddar
  cheese

Spoon Rolls

- ▼ Dissolve the yeast in the lukewarm water in a large bowl.
- ▼ Add the egg, margarine and sugar and mix well.
- ▼ Stir in the flour gradually, mixing well after each addition. Drop the dough by spoonfuls into greased muffin cups.
- ▼ Bake at 425 degrees for about 20 minutes or until golden brown.

Yield: 24 rolls

1 envelope dry yeast
2 cups lukewarm water
1 egg, beaten
$3/4$ cup melted margarine or
  butter
$1/4$ cup sugar
4 cups self-rising flour

German Chocolate Upside-Down Cake

2 tablespoons melted margarine
1 cup chopped pecans
1 (6-ounce) package frozen
  shredded coconut
1 (2-layer) package German
  chocolate cake mix
8 ounces cream cheese, softened
1 (1-pound) package
  confectioners' sugar

▼ Pour the margarine into a greased 9x13-inch cake pan.
▼ Sprinkle the pecans and coconut evenly in the pan.
▼ Prepare the cake mix according to the package directions. Pour the batter carefully over the pecans and coconut.
▼ Beat the cream cheese and confectioners' sugar in a bowl until smooth.
▼ Spread the cream cheese mixture evenly over the batter.
▼ Bake at 350 degrees for 45 to 50 minutes or until the cake tests done.
▼ Cool on a wire rack.
▼ Cut the cake into squares. Invert onto dessert plates.
▼ May serve with ice cream or whipped topping.

Yield: 18 to 21 squares

Easy Lemon Cookies

1 egg
2 cups whipped topping
1 (2-layer) package lemon cake
  mix
Confectioners' sugar

▼ Beat the egg lightly in a large bowl. Add the whipped topping and blend well. Add the cake mix and mix well.
▼ Place a generous amount of confectioners' sugar in a shallow bowl.
▼ Drop the cookie dough by teaspoonfuls into the confectioners' sugar and roll into a ball. The dough is very soft so you may wish to use spoons to roll and coat the dough.
▼ Arrange the balls on a lightly greased cookie sheet.
▼ Bake at 350 degrees for 10 to 12 minutes or until brown.
▼ Cool on the cookie sheet for 1 minute. Remove to a wire rack to cool completely.

Yield: 24 cookies

Hello Dollies

▼ Melt the margarine in a 9x13-inch baking pan.
▼ Sprinkle the graham cracker crumbs evenly over the melted margarine and press over the bottom of the pan.
▼ Drizzle the condensed milk over the crumb layer.
▼ Add layers of chocolate chips, coconut and pecans and pat lightly.
▼ Bake at 350 degrees for 25 minutes.
▼ Cool in the pan on a wire rack.
▼ Cut into squares.

Yield: 24 to 36 cookies

1/2 **cup margarine**
1 1/2 **cups graham cracker crumbs**
1 **(14-ounce) can sweetened condensed milk**
1 **cup chocolate chips**
1 **(3-ounce) can shredded coconut**
1 **to** 1 1/2 **cups chopped pecans**

Quick Banana Shake

▼ Combine the milk and maple syrup in a blender container.
▼ Crush the graham crackers and add to the blender.
▼ Slice the banana and add to the blender container.
▼ Process for 30 seconds or until smooth and well blended.
▼ Serve immediately.

Yield: 1 serving

1 **cup skim milk**
2 **tablespoons maple syrup or honey**
6 **graham crackers**
1 **banana**

Lighthouse

Light Fare

Lighthouse

Built to replace the ineffective Cumberland Island Light, the Amelia Island Lighthouse was completed and lighted in 1839. It is the oldest documented structure on Amelia Island. Congress approved the petition for the new light in March of 1837 and appropriated eight thousand dollars for the construction on five acres of marshfront land. The sixty-foot structure is located on a high ridge, probably formed by a line of ancient sand dunes. At an elevation of 107 feet above sea level, the light can be seen nineteen miles at sea.

The lighthouse has a base of red brick walls four feet thick, tapering as it rises. There are sixty-nine winding steps of granite, hand-hewn and shipped here from New England, leading up from the base to the rotating mechanism. The original light was fueled with whale oil. Early keepers climbed those sixty-nine steps twice daily in order to extinguish the lamp each morning and to light the lamp each evening.

Cantaloupe Soup

▼ Cut the melon into halves. Scoop out and discard the seeds and pulp. Peel the cantaloupe and cut the melon flesh into cubes.

▼ Place the melon cubes in a blender container. Process until puréed.

▼ Add the orange juice, ½ cup yogurt and lime juice. Process until smooth. Pour into a bowl.

▼ Chill for several hours.

▼ Pour the cold soup into soup bowls.

▼ Top with a dollop of about ½ tablespoon yogurt and fresh mint leaves.

Yield: 4 to 6 servings

1 large ripe cantaloupe
1 cup fresh orange juice
½ cup plain yogurt
1 tablespoon fresh lime juice
2 to 3 tablespoons plain yogurt
Fresh mint leaves

Gazpacho

▼ Combine the tomatoes, cucumber, onion, green pepper, parsley, garlic, salt and pepper in a food processor container.

▼ Process until the vegetables are chopped into small pieces.

▼ Stir in the vinegar and olive oil.

▼ Refrigerate for 1 hour or until chilled through.

Yield: 4 servings

4 large tomatoes, peeled
½ cucumber, peeled, seeded
½ Vidalia onion
¼ green bell pepper
3 tablespoons parsley
1½ teaspoons finely chopped garlic
1 teaspoon (or less) salt
1 teaspoon pepper
3 tablespoons red wine vinegar
1 tablespoon olive oil

Mushroom and Potato Chowder

1 small onion, chopped
1 rib celery, chopped
1/2 small green bell pepper, chopped
8 ounces fresh mushrooms, sliced
2 tablespoons butter or margarine
2 cups chopped peeled red potatoes
2 cups chicken broth
1/2 teaspoon thyme
1 1/2 cups milk
1/2 teaspoon salt
1/2 teaspoon pepper
1/2 cup milk
3 tablespoons flour

▼ Sauté the onion, celery, green pepper and mushrooms in the butter in a large soup pot until tender.

▼ Add the potatoes, chicken broth and thyme. Bring to a boil and reduce the heat.

▼ Simmer, uncovered, for 30 minutes or until the potatoes are tender, stirring occasionally.

▼ Stir in 1 1/2 cups milk, salt and pepper.

▼ Blend the remaining 1/2 cup milk with the flour. Stir into the soup.

▼ Simmer, uncovered, until slightly thickened, stirring frequently.

Yield: 4 to 6 servings

Low-Calorie Vegetable Soup

▼ Combine the vegetable juice and undrained canned vegetables in a large soup pot.

▼ Add the bouillon cube. Bring the mixture to a boil, stirring until the bouillon cube dissolves.

▼ Add the potatoes, onions, carrots and Worcestershire sauce and mix well. Return to a boil and reduce the heat.

▼ Simmer, covered, for 1 to 1½ hours, stirring occasionally.

Yield: 8 to 10 servings

1 (46-ounce) can vegetable juice cocktail
1 (16-ounce) can green beans
1 (14-ounce) can whole kernel corn
1 beef bouillon cube
4 medium Irish potatoes, peeled, chopped
4 medium onions, chopped
4 carrots, sliced
1 tablespoon Worcestershire sauce

Watch Your Step

A bad crack, which the Coast Guard attributes to the 1898 hurricane, scissors through the granite steps of the lighthouse up to the light. A former lighthouse keeper, the late Tom O'Hagan used to say that some early keeper wound the clock too tight and the cable broke, sending the weight crashing down to the steps below. Whatever the cause, the crack is now held together by a strip of bolted iron.

Dilled Shrimp and Feta Cheese Salad

1 quart water
1 pound large shrimp, peeled, deveined
3 green onions with tops, thinly sliced
½ medium cucumber, peeled, seeded, chopped
2 tablespoons snipped fresh dill
¼ cup crumbled feta cheese
2 tablespoons lemon juice
2 tablespoons olive oil
1 tablespoon white wine vinegar
1 teaspoon Dijon mustard
1 clove of garlic, minced
¼ teaspoon pepper

▼ Bring 1 quart water to a boil in a large saucepan. Add the shrimp.

▼ Cook for 2 minutes or until the shrimp are firm and turn pink.

▼ Drain the shrimp immediately and rinse under cold running water to stop the cooking.

▼ Drain the shrimp well and place in a bowl.

▼ Add the green onions, cucumber, dill and feta cheese.

▼ Combine the lemon juice, olive oil, wine vinegar, mustard, garlic and pepper in a small bowl and whisk until well mixed.

▼ Pour the dressing over the shrimp mixture and toss to mix.

Yield: 4 servings

A Difficult Task

The toughest chore for the lighthouse keeper was winding the clock cables with those heavy weights. Polishing the brass and glass cleaning were done each week. Glass cleaning was a rather dangerous chore as rays of sunlight shining through the lens could burn skin!

Barbecued Beef

▼ Cut the beef into 2-inch chunks. Brown the chunks on all sides in a large nonstick skillet. Place in a baking dish.

▼ Sauté the onion in the oil in the skillet for 3 minutes.

▼ Add the vinegar, chili sauce, tomato sauce, chili powder, Worcestershire sauce, sugar, thyme, tomatoes, broth and wine and mix well.

▼ Bring the mixture to a boil and pour over the beef.

▼ Bake, covered, at 300 degrees for 2½ hours or until the beef falls apart in shreds when pierced with a fork.

▼ Shred the beef and mix well with the sauce.

▼ Serve on toasted buns.

Yield: 8 servings

2 pounds top round
1 cup chopped onion
1 teaspoon vegetable oil
½ cup white wine vinegar
¼ cup chili sauce
¼ cup tomato sauce
2 teaspoons chili powder
2 teaspoons Worcestershire sauce
2 teaspoons sugar
¼ teaspoon thyme
1 cup stewed tomatoes
½ cup beef broth
½ cup red wine
8 buns, toasted

Black Bean Lasagna

2 (16-ounce) cans black beans
1 cup salsa
2 cups meatless spaghetti sauce
1 large clove of garlic, minced
1 teaspoon cumin
1 (15-ounce) carton nonfat
   ricotta cheese
½ cup grated Parmesan cheese
2 egg whites, or ¼ cup egg
   substitute
6 lasagna noodles
1 cup shredded part-skim
   mozzarella cheese

▼ Drain the beans, rinse and drain well. Place the beans in a large bowl and mash.

▼ Add the salsa, spaghetti sauce, garlic and cumin. Mix well and set aside.

▼ Combine the ricotta cheese, Parmesan cheese and egg whites in a medium bowl. Mix well and set aside.

▼ Soak the lasagna noodles in very hot water for several minutes. (This is not necessary if using no-cook noodles.)

▼ Spray a 9x13-inch baking dish with nonstick cooking spray. Drain the noodles.

▼ Spread 1 cup of the bean mixture in the prepared dish. Arrange 3 of the noodles in the dish.

▼ Add layers of half the remaining bean mixture, half the ricotta cheese mixture and half the mozzarella cheese.

▼ Repeat the layers with the remaining noodles, bean mixture, ricotta cheese mixture and mozzarella cheese.

▼ Bake, covered with foil, at 350 degrees for 25 minutes.

▼ Uncover and bake for 5 minutes longer.

▼ Let stand for 5 minutes before serving.

Yield: 8 servings

Variation: For **Microwave Black Bean Lasagna**, prepare and assemble the lasagna as above. Cut several long slits about ½ inch deep in the top of the lasagna. Cover with plastic wrap. Microwave on High for 16 to 18 minutes, turning twice. Let stand for 5 minutes before serving.

Dieter's Boiled Shrimp and White Sauce for Pasta

▼ Bring the broth to a simmer in a medium saucepan.

▼ Cut the cheese into pieces and add to the hot broth. Cook over low heat until the cheese melts, stirring constantly. Add the garlic and onion powder and mix well.

▼ Add the shrimp. Heat to serving temperature, stirring frequently.

▼ Cook the pasta according to the package directions. Drain and place in a large bowl.

▼ Add the sauce and Parmesan cheese and toss to mix.

▼ Serve immediately.

Yield: 4 servings

Variation: Substitute sautéed shrimp, cooked crab meat, cooked chicken or steamed vegetables for the boiled shrimp. Add the desired amount of Parmesan cheese to the sauce.

1 (12-ounce) can chicken broth
12 ounces Neufchâtel or fat-free cream cheese, softened
Garlic and onion powder to taste
1 pound peeled boiled shrimp
12 ounces angel hair pasta
Parmesan cheese to taste

Pasta Puttanesca

1 (28-ounce) can crushed Italian
   tomatoes or stewed tomatoes,
   chopped
1/2 cup (or less) sliced black olives
1 tablespoon capers
1 1/2 tablespoons olive oil
1 clove of garlic, crushed
2 or 3 fresh plum tomatoes,
   chopped
Fresh basil, parsley and oregano
   to taste
Salt and pepper to taste
16 ounces favorite pasta

▼ Combine the canned tomatoes, olives, capers, olive oil, garlic and fresh tomatoes in a large bowl or saucepan.

▼ Add the basil, parsley and oregano in any combination or proportion. Add the salt and pepper.

▼ Let the mixture stand at room temperature to blend the flavors.

▼ Cook the pasta al dente according to the package directions.

▼ Drain the pasta and place in a large bowl. Add the desired amount of room temperature sauce and toss to mix.

▼ Serve immediately.

Yield: 6 servings

Variation: Heat the sauce to serving temperature before adding to the pasta.

No Shipwreck Wanted

The Lighthouse Beacon is currently powered by four 1000-watt lamps. The light burns continuously, with the one-minute revolution of lens and prisms creating a flashing effect. A red sector flashes danger, a warning that ships are too close to shore.

Vegetable Lasagna Guilt-Free

This recipe has been concocted and fine-tuned with the help of a garden full of squash. The moisture in the vegetables is enough to cook the noodles. If using a pan too small to hold the whole noodles, just soak the noodles in hot water for about ten minutes to make pliable and cut to fit.

2 or 3 yellow squash
2 or 3 zucchini
Salt to taste
8 ounces fresh mushrooms
10 ounces fresh or frozen spinach
1 (15-ounce) can tomato sauce
9 to 12 lasagna noodles
4 green onions with tops, chopped
Canned water-pack artichoke hearts to taste
Chopped black olives to taste
16 ounces cottage cheese
1 or 2 fresh tomatoes, sliced
Shredded mozzarella cheese to taste

▼ Slice the squash and zucchini ¼ inch thick into rounds. Place on a large microwave-safe plate and salt lightly. Microwave just until crisply limp and set aside.

▼ Slice the mushrooms. Place on a large microwave-safe plate and salt lightly. Microwave as with the squash.

▼ Rinse the spinach well, discard the stems and microwave just until wilted. (If using frozen spinach, thaw, drain and squeeze almost dry.)

▼ Spray a lasagna pan with nonstick cooking spray. Spread about 2 tablespoons of the tomato sauce over the bottom of the pan. Reserve several tablespoons of the tomato sauce. Reserve enough noodles to use as a topping.

▼ Layer 3 of the remaining uncooked lasagna noodles and ⅓ to ½ of the squash, zucchini, green onions, spinach, artichoke hearts, olives, tomato sauce and cottage cheese in the prepared pan.

▼ Repeat the layers 2 or 3 times, ending with the reserved noodles. Spread the reserved tomato sauce over the noodles.

▼ Arrange overlapping slices of the tomatoes over the noodles, covering completely.

▼ Bake, covered with foil, at 350 degrees for 30 minutes.

▼ Remove the foil and sprinkle with the desired amount of mozzarella cheese.

▼ Bake, uncovered, for 10 minutes longer.

Yield: 6 to 8 servings

Vegetarian Manicotti

12 ounces fresh tofu, mashed
2¹/₂ cups low-fat cottage cheese
1 medium onion, finely chopped
3 tablespoons chopped fresh
parsley
3 egg whites
¹/₄ cup bread crumbs
20 uncooked manicotti shells
Zesty Pasta Sauce

The sauce is also excellent served over spaghetti.

▼ Combine the tofu, cottage cheese, onion, parsley, egg whites and bread crumbs in a bowl and mix well.
▼ Stuff the tofu mixture into the uncooked manicotti shells.
▼ Pour 1 cup Zesty Pasta Sauce into each of two 7x11-inch baking dishes.
▼ Arrange the stuffed manicotti in a single layer in the prepared pans.
▼ Spoon the remaining sauce over the manicotti.
▼ Bake, covered with foil, at 350 degrees for 50 to 60 minutes or until the manicotti shells are tender.

Zesty Pasta Sauce

2 (16-ounce) cans tomatoes,
chopped
2 (6-ounce) cans tomato paste
2 medium onions, chopped
2 large green bell peppers, finely
chopped
4 cloves of garlic, minced
¹/₂ cup chopped fresh parsley
¹/₄ cup sugar
1 teaspoon dried oregano
2 teaspoons dried basil
¹/₂ teaspoon pepper
2 bay leaves
¹/₂ cup dry red wine
4 cups water

▼ Combine the undrained tomatoes and tomato paste in a large nonstick skillet.
▼ Add the onions, green peppers, garlic, parsley, sugar, oregano, basil, pepper and bay leaves and mix well. Stir in the wine and water.
▼ Bring to a boil, stirring frequently. Reduce the heat to a simmer and cover.
▼ Simmer for 2 hours, stirring occasionally.
▼ Discard the bay leaves.

Yield: 10 servings

Vegetarian Pizza

▼ Peel the eggplant and slice thinly.

▼ Sauté the eggplant, onion, green pepper and mushrooms in the olive oil in a large skillet over low heat. Drain and set aside.

▼ Combine the cottage cheese with the pesto in a small bowl and mix well.

▼ Spread the cottage cheese mixture over the pizza crust very thinly.

▼ Add the sautéed vegetables in a thin layer.

▼ Top with the cheeses.

▼ Place the pizza crust directly on the oven rack in a preheated 425-degree oven.

▼ Bake for 10 minutes or until the cheese is melted and bubbly.

Yield: 4 servings

Variation: Substitute 2 cloves of garlic and 6 fresh basil leaves that have been finely chopped for the pesto.

1/2 **eggplant**
1/2 **medium onion, chopped**
1/4 **green bell pepper, chopped**
1 **cup sliced mushrooms**
1 **tablespoon (or more) olive oil**
1/2 **to 1 cup fat-free cottage cheese**
3 **tablespoons pesto**
1 **large gourmet pizza crust**
3/4 **cup grated Parmesan cheese**
3/4 **cup shredded mozzarella cheese**

Tomato and Basil Pie

1 refrigerated all ready pie crust
8 plum tomatoes
¹/₂ cup fat-free cottage cheese
3 cloves of garlic, minced
6 fresh basil leaves, minced
¹/₂ cup grated Parmesan cheese
³/₄ cup shredded mozzarella
cheese

▼ Let the pie crust stand at room temperature for several minutes to soften.
▼ Fit the pie crust into an ungreased pie plate. Flute the edge and pierce with a fork in several places.
▼ Slice the tomatoes ¹/₈ to ¹/₄ inch thick.
▼ Combine the cottage cheese, garlic and basil in a small bowl and mix well. Spread the mixture over the bottom of the pie crust.
▼ Arrange overlapping tomato slices over the cottage cheese mixture.
▼ Sprinkle with the Parmesan and mozzarella cheeses.
▼ Bake at 400 degrees for 30 minutes or until the cheeses bubble and the crust is golden brown.

Yield: 4 entrée servings or 6 side dish servings

Baked Mushroom Rice

2 cups uncooked long grain rice
1 cup sliced green onions
2 tablespoons butter or margarine
3 cups chicken broth
1 (4-ounce) jar sliced mushrooms
1 (4-ounce) jar chopped
pimentos, drained
1 teaspoon salt
1 teaspoon seasoned pepper

▼ Place the rice in a lightly greased 7x11-inch baking dish.
▼ Sauté the green onions in butter in a large skillet over medium-high heat until tender.
▼ Stir in the broth, undrained mushrooms, pimentos, salt and pepper.
▼ Bring to a boil and pour over the rice.
▼ Bake, covered, at 375 degrees for 25 minutes or until the liquid is absorbed and the rice is tender.
▼ Stir and fluff the rice before serving.

Yield: 8 servings

Stuffed Zucchini

▼ Cut the zucchini into halves lengthwise. Scoop out the pulp, forming ¼-inch-thick shells.

▼ Chop the zucchini pulp. Set the zucchini shells aside.

▼ Sauté the zucchini pulp, onion, garlic, mushrooms and sunflower seed kernels in the butter in a large skillet until tender. Season with rosemary, basil and thyme.

▼ Combine the brown rice, cottage cheese, eggs, wheat germ, soy sauce, Tabasco sauce and Worcestershire sauce in a large bowl and mix well.

▼ Add the sautéed vegetables and the cheese and mix well.

▼ Spoon the mixture into the zucchini shells. Sprinkle with paprika.

▼ Place in a lightly greased 9x13-inch baking dish.

▼ Bake at 350 degrees for 40 minutes or until the zucchini shells are tender.

Yield: 6 servings

3 medium zucchini
1 large onion, chopped
1 clove of garlic, minced
8 ounces mushrooms, chopped
2 tablespoons sunflower seed kernels (optional)
2 tablespoons butter
¼ teaspoon each dried rosemary, basil and thyme
1 cup cooked brown rice
1½ cups cottage cheese
3 eggs, beaten
¼ cup wheat germ
3 tablespoons soy sauce
2 dashes of Tabasco sauce
1 dash of Worcestershire sauce
1 cup shredded Cheddar cheese
Paprika to taste

Overnight French Toast

▼ Mix the eggs, milk, orange juice, zest and vanilla in a bowl until well blended. Pour into a shallow baking pan.

▼ Slice the bread 1 inch thick. Place the bread slices in the baking pan, turning to coat the slices.

▼ Cover the pan with plastic wrap and refrigerate overnight. Remove the bread slices to a greased baking sheet.

▼ Bake at 375 degrees for 20 to 25 minutes or until golden brown. Serve with maple syrup or honey.

Yield: 6 servings

12 eggs or equivalent egg substitute
½ cup low-fat milk
2 tablespoons orange juice
Grated zest of 1 orange
½ teaspoon vanilla extract
1 loaf French bread

Contributor List

Carrie Allen
Georgia Allen
Joyce Allen
Carol Altman
Tricia Alvarez
Cindy Austin
Sally Bailey
Julie Ballard
Steve Ballard
Vicki Beaudry
Shirley Bolden
Jan Brogdon
Barbara Bruce
Sandye Brunson
Bill Bryan
Chris Bryan
Sandy Burch
Marie Carman
Brenda Carr
Sandra Carver
Anne Childers
Marcia Cline
Ray Cline
Frances Colson
Lorraine Corbett
Laverne Craig
Cyndy Cunningham
Peggy Dennard
Dale Deonas
Mary Martha Embry

Sally Ericksen
Liz Evans
Marian Ferris
Carol Floyd
Patty Fowler
Boots Gass
Mickie Griffin-Nelson
Pawnee Hall
Paul Harrell
Lisa Harter
Barbara Heymann
Stephanie Hickox
Lynn Hicks
Alice Holton
Marie Homan
Patty House
Brian Kendall
Pam Knight
Barbara LaBonte
Flo Lane
Cindy Leary
Amy Lemery
Diane Lindorff
Debbie Little
Shelly Macomber
Paula Margiotta
Eddie McKendree
Joanne McRae
Jo Mirschel
Martha Lee Mitchell

Menza Mitchell
Rhonda Murray
Linda Neal
Lou Nelson
Winette Odom
Shirley Owens
June Peters
Shirley Peters
Jean Peterson
Heather Rodeffer
Marolyn Rogers
Kathy Rogers-Shanks
Barbara Trapp Ross
Marvalene Sage
Nan Sands
Bill Scholz
Pamela Selton
Joan Sheets
Katherine Shipman
Linda Southwell
Gina Taylor
Bonnie Tennille
Mildred Thomas
Lynn Todd
Barbi Townsend
Amy Wampler
Rebecca Westendorff
Melba Whitaker
Paige Whitaker
Suzanne Willis

Index